Jolanta Soysal
MY SONG

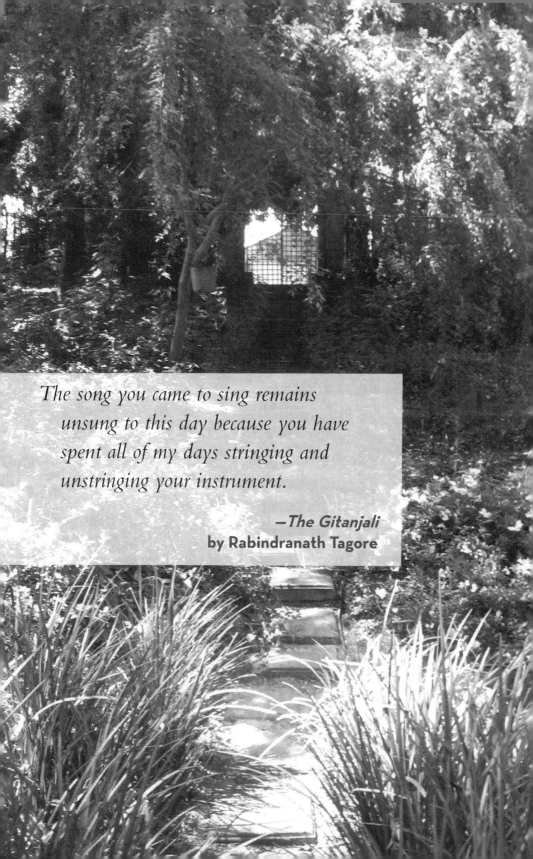

The song you came to sing remains
unsung to this day because you have
spent all of my days stringing and
unstringing your instrument.

—*The Gitanjali*
by **Rabindranath Tagore**

Jolanta Soysal
MY SONG

with Tom Bleecker

Gilderoy
Publications

Gilderoy Publications
Menifee, California

Gilderoy Publications titles are available at quantity discounts for sales
promotions, premiums or fund raising. For information, contact Gilderoy Publications at Gilderoy@aol.com

Library of Congress Cataloging-in-Publication Data

Soysal, Jolanta 1944-
Jolanta Soysal, My Song / Jolanta Soysal with Tom Bleecker /
p.cm.
ISBN 978-0-9653132-6-1 (tradepaper)
Jolanta Soysal 1944—. Poland—Immigration—biography. I. Bleecker,
Tom. II. My Song.

1st printing, August 2015

The paper used in this publication meets the minimum requirements
of the American National Standard for Information Sciences—Performance of Paper for Printed Library Materials, ANSI Z39.48-1984.
Printed in the United States of America

Cover and book design by: Kurt Wahlner

To my mother—

my greatest pillar in life,

and for all her years of love,

worry, wisdom, and guidance

that helped shape me into

the best person I could become.

Her loving memory will reside

in my heart until we are reunited

for eternity.

CONTENTS

"All the News That's Fit to Print"

The New York Times.

EXTRA

GERMAN ARMY ATTACKS POLAND;
CITIES BOMBED, PORT BLOCKADED;
DANZIG IS ACCEPTED INTO REICH

The *New York Times* headlines September 1, 1939.

CHAPTER ONE

POLAND

I n the fall of 1939, the people of Poland lived in a peaceful, democratic society. That changed on September 1, 1939 when Germany invaded Poland without warning or a formal declaration of war, triggering the start of World War Two.

Bialystok is located on the banks of the Biała River in northeastern Poland and is characterized by warm summers, thick forests, and long frosty winters. In 1939, Bialystok was predominantly Jewish, although the city was a religiously diverse society in which Jewish, Christian Orthodox, Protestant, and Roman Catholic groups coexisted.

The German invasion of Poland was followed two weeks later by an invasion by the Soviet Union (USSR). Within days, Warsaw capitulated. Throughout the course of foreign occupation that ended in May 1945, Poland was divided between Nazi Germany and the Soviet Union. Both occupying powers were hostile to the existence of a sovereign Poland, Polish culture, and the Polish people, aiming at their destruction.

From the beginning, the Nazis pursued a ruthless policy of pillage and removal of the non-German population. In August 1941, the 56,000 Jewish residents of Bialystok were herded into a small area of the city and confined in a ghetto. Most inmates were put to work in the forced-labor enterprises for the German war effort, primarily in large textile, shoe, and chemical factories established within its boundaries. Throughout the occupation, millions of ordinary Poles—at great risk to themselves and their families—engaged in rescuing a half-million Jews from the German Nazis.

German troops parade through Warsaw after invasion of Poland.

ABOVE: Polish kid in the ruins of Warsaw. LEFT: German concentration camp in Poland.

In 1943 my parents Bruno and Helen Kurstak lived in Bialystok where they sheltered a Jewish woman, who was their friend. My parents didn't care what religion she was. One day, the German Gestapo, following an informant tip, came to my parents' house and arrested the woman and my parents. In the ensuing hours of interrogation by the Nazis, my father was beaten so badly that he lost consciousness. He awoke the following day in a work camp in Germany where the harsh conditions and treatment he endured were inhumane.

Polish Jews transported to holding areas.

Because my mother was two months pregnant, the Germans took her to their newly-constructed ghetto in Bialystok. She was an intelligent person who knew how to read situations. Although she didn't speak German, one day in September of 1943 she noticed movement and became convinced that the Germans were about to move the ghetto, most likely to Auschwitz where she knew, because of her pregnancy, she would be first in line for extermination.

At great risk, she wrote a generic letter to a friend and went to one of several guardhouses. Showing the letter to the guards, she said, "I'm just going to mail this letter." When the guards allowed her to pass, she walked slowly for a half hour, holding the letter high in the air for all to see, praying that she wouldn't be shot in the back. Once far out of sight of the ghetto, she tore the Jewish star from her coat and traveled only at nighttime. After three days, she arrived at the home of my father's parents in Kurczowce where she stayed in hiding. Not knowing what had become of my father, she had little choice but to wait there for him.

After my father recovered from his injuries, he managed to escape from the work camp and traveled only at night, sleeping in freshly dug graves. Because it was now the dead of winter in which the temperature fell below freezing, he lost several of his toes to frostbite. After traveling for six months, his body finally collapsed in the snow, accepting death.

Fortunately, a group of sympathetic communists discovered his near-frozen body and took him to a nearby house where he received care. After recuperating for several weeks, he traveled to the home of his parents where he was reunited with my mother. Because each had assumed the other had died, they were overjoyed to see one another. Adding to their glorious reunion, days later on March 17, 1944 my mother gave birth to me.

Shortly after I was born, the communists took over the part of Poland where my father's parents lived, causing my parents to return to Bialystok where, because the Germans had left, they felt the family would be safe. As a historical footnote, by the time the Germans were defeated, they had murdered six million Polish citizens—nearly a quarter of Poland's population—who died between 1939 and 1945 as a result of the Nazi occupation, half of whom were Polish Jews.

When the war ended in 1945, Poland, although now under control of the Soviet Union, again became a democracy with free elections. Although Soviet Premier Joseph Stalin made guarantees to the leaders of the free world—Prime Minister Winston Churchill and President Franklin Roosevelt—that the Soviet Union would maintain Poland's sovereignty and allow democratic elections to take place, the elections organized by the occupying com-

ABOVE: Bialystok ghetto. BELOW: Jewish Ghetto Police.

munist authorities were falsified. As a result, the Soviet Union installed a new communist government in Poland that answered directly to Moscow and was analogous to much of the rest of the Eastern Bloc.

Over the next four decades, the vast majority of Polish citizens never felt part of the Soviet Bloc. Although we were occupied by the communists and our government officials took orders from the USSR, we weren't willing participants.

CHAPTER TWO

CHILDHOOD

Immediately following the end of World War II, although the killing on both sides had ended, the political differences between the leaders of the Free World and the Soviet Union had in no way subsided. What had been a "hot war" was being continued as what was now commonly accepted as a "Cold War."

In a blatant display of saber rattling and flexing the muscle of the Free World, in January 1950, US President Truman made it known that he had ordered the development of the hydrogen bomb, which was five times the explosive power of either of the two atomic bombs that were dropped on Japan five years earlier. Undeterred, in June of that same year, North Korea attacked South Korea, igniting the start of the Korean War.

Adding fuel to this new hot war, US Senator Joseph McCarthy launched a witch hunt for communist spies he was convinced were residing in the United States. In short order, in March 1951, Julius and Ethel Rosenberg were sentenced to death in the United States for passing atomic secrets to the Soviet Union. Soon thereafter, the Soviet Union announced it had exploded a hydrogen bomb. On both sides of the world, nuclear warheads were being constructed at an alarming rate, and absolutely no one anywhere was to be trusted.

My mother gave birth to four children. The first was a boy, who was born at home and sorrowfully died from an infection when he was only a few weeks old. I was my mother's second

From left: my sister Halina, my mother, my sister Alicja, and me.

child, and was followed four years later by my sister Halina, and then four years after Halina's birth, my sister Alicja was born.

I was my mother's favorite child because I often spent time with her doing her household chores. Because she had endured so much escaping from the Bialystok ghetto and hiding from the Germans, she often said to me, "I know you'll be a fighter in life because of everything I went through to bring you into the world."

Unlike me, my sisters preferred to spend time with their friends and had little time to talk with our mother. We did, however, make sure that we were home on time, which was vitally important to my father. When I was so much as ten minutes late, he would lock the doors and make me sleep outside, getting up every half hour to check on me.

Because my father was an only child, he was doted on by his mother, who made a point of dressing him in a suit, making sure his hair was trimmed, and that he smelled of her favorite cologne. From the moment he awoke in the morning until the moment he fell off to sleep at night, he was pampered like a crown prince. Although his family wasn't rich, unlike most Poles, they owned land and lived a lifestyle above the norm.

As a child, I resented my father because I felt that he took my mother for granted. To him, his wife had taken over the duties of his mother in treating him like royalty. As is often the case with a relationship based on servitude, my father was not emotionally available to my mother and rarely displayed signs of affection or words of gratitude.

During meals he had his own personal silverware. He'd sit at the head of the table and call out, "Helen, Helen, where's my spoon?" and "Helen, where's my fork?" Although his regularly polished silverware was five feet away from him in a cabinet, he felt retrieving it was one of my mother's many duties. In my eyes, he was a moody, selfish baby who felt that his needs should come before everyone else's. When he used the bathroom, he took an hour to shave and comb his hair. He was like an old lady. In a sense, I felt that my father came off as being handicapped.

As a growing child I felt that that my father was disappointed with me and my sisters because he wanted a boy and instead ended up with three girls. The fact that my mother had given birth to a boy who had died shortly after birth further frustrated my father. Although he was never physically abusive, he was short-tempered and often criticized me. At night before retiring, although I would routinely kiss my mother goodnight, my father preferred that to him I only *say* goodnight.

Besides being a devoutly religious person who prayed daily, thanking God for her family's good health and their daily blessings, my mother placed a high value on family unity and brought the family together whenever she could. One of her special gatherings was mealtimes. We'd all sit together at the family table for breakfast and supper, which were light meals, and dinner, which was our family's biggest meal. My mother didn't care what plans we had during the day, she wanted us home for meals.

As a child, I disliked food and dreaded being called to the family table for meals. Because my father loved to eat, my mother made enough food to satisfy a king's appetite, which meant there was more than enough for us kids. Unlike my two sisters, I had practically no appetite, which resulted in my being skinny and my father constantly insisting that I eat. After months of my continuing to hold out, my parents began to occasionally pay me to eat. I'd earn the Polish currency equivalent of a dime for breakfast, 15 cents for supper, and a quarter for dinner. While this money making business annoyed my father, my sisters were in favor of it because I often spent the money I earned on them.

I kept my resentment toward my father to myself. I didn't voice my disdain toward him outside our home because my mother had instilled in me at an early age that it was wrong to say anything negative to anyone about one's family. "It's our nest," she often said. "What happens in our house is between us and is nobody's business." As a child, if I was unhappy about something,

I kept it to myself and as I grew older had a strong tendency to hold everything in.

After the war ended, the majority of food that was produced in Poland was sent to the Soviet Union, and as a result, Poland often was faced with food shortages. My mother was an extremely resourceful person and would travel to the village to buy a pig, then return home and spend days making sausages and cold cuts that would last our family for an entire month. Unlike many homes in Poland, we had a stockpile of food because my mother worked hard to provide a better life for her family. She was our heart and soul, and in my mind there wasn't anything she couldn't do. Profoundly generous, she never turned away anyone in need if there was a way she could help. She made life seem so easy that I felt that my life would be trouble free if I all I did was be the way my mother was and did what she did. She was the consummate role model and I felt totally protected and secure when I was with her.

After World War II ended and throughout the Cold War, people in the United States believed, most likely through propaganda, that people who lived in Poland, because we were part of the Soviet Bloc, were sad-faced, downtrodden, physically overweight, and wore drab clothing. While this may have been partially true of citizens living in the Soviet Union, this wasn't the case throughout much of Poland whose people still envisioned themselves as living in a free, democratic society, regardless of our being ruled by the communists.

By common postwar standards, my family was comfortable. Much like the United States, our home was heated by coal and powered by electricity. Unlike most homes in America, however, we didn't have a refrigerator. Instead, we refrigerated our food in the basement, which was the coldest part of the house, and had fresh milk delivered daily. Because my mother cooked homemade meals three times a day, having a refrigerator wasn't necessary.

We also didn't have a washing machine and dryer. My mother washed all our clothes by hand and dried them outside on the line during the summer and by our furnace in wintertime. Every Saturday we had fresh linens that were ironed and smelled like country air.

One of several focal points in our home was a radio that we would sit in front of and listen to. Several times a week, I'd run home from school so that I would be on time to listen to the violinist-composer Henryk Wieniawski, who was born in Lubin, Poland. To this day, I become mesmerized listening to recordings of his violin and viola. As a footnote, Wieniawski was given a number of posthumous honors. His portrait appeared on a postage stamp of Poland in 1952 and again in 1957. A 100 złoty coin was issued in 1979 bearing his image. From an early age I developed a love of music thanks to our family's radio.

The communists authorized everything that went over the airwaves. Because our radio was equipped with a special antenna, my parents sometimes listened to Radio Free Europe that provided news and information to countries in Eastern Europe, Central Asia, and the Middle East where the free flow of information was either banned by government authorities or not fully developed. Sometimes at night, I could hear my parents talking in the living room about what they were hearing on the radio. Although I was too young to understand the politics of what my parents were discussing, it was clear to me that my mother tended to be open-minded toward what she was hearing about the Free World, while my father was anything but.

Besides school athletics, I had access to what was called a "Communist Center" where I developed ballet, painting, and singing. I was constantly at this center because it was within walking distance from my home. When I entered my teens, my parents weren't fond of my participating in sports because practices took time away from my being at home where my mother had gotten used to my helping with her cleaning. Before long, I became obsessed with sports and was constantly coming home with injuries and ripped clothing. From an early age, I loved competing in sports, which was encouraged by the communists who were

Age 13 wearing
a vest that I
made and with
new hairstyle
for the
photographer.

Age 15 in high school.

determined that its citizens outdo everyone. This was particularly evident in the Olympics, which for decades were dominated by the communists. In sharp contrast to the United States, however, the communist system has always been highly opposed to any athlete being paid the outlandish sums of money that are earned by professional athletes in America.

For the most part, I enjoyed my years in high school and did well scholastically, although I didn't like to study. Fortunately, I was extremely creative and could think on my feet, to quote an old cliché—which was a characteristic that carried into my adult years. One of many examples was the morning my creative writing teacher called on me to read my story (which was my homework assignment from the previous day) to the class. Rather than tell the teacher I hadn't done my homework, I stood before the class and read five blank pages, at the end of which the teacher praised my "beautiful story" and gave me an "A."

My sisters and I attended public school because after the war private schools no longer existed in Poland. While I wanted to stand out in school so that my mother would be proud of me, besides doing well scholastically, I excelled in sports and was a fierce competitor who was driven to win at all costs. No doubt this was because as a child I had been a tomboy at heart. Besides doing well scholastically and on the athletic fields, I had a knack for charming my teachers so much and so often that when they met with my mother they couldn't say enough nice things about me.

I was by no means a perfect child, which I credit to my having an inborn dislike for rules. Although I admired and respected my mother, on occasion I became a major headache. One such annoyance was that I liked to hide from her and make her come looking for me, sometimes even at night and even away from our home.

One night when I was ten, I snuck out my bedroom window and ended up walking through the park. Part of what drove me to do this was a sense of adventure coupled with a curiosity about what people did at night. As I continued along listening to the

High School ROTC (I hid behind a fellow student).

sounds of the night, I wondered if this was the way my mother had felt when she was traveling at night running from the Germans. After several moments passed, I began singing, quietly at first, and then louder. Suddenly someone began clapping in the darkness. I instantly became frightened and wanted to yell out for my mother. After a long while of contemplating the air, I whispered anxiously, "Oh, my God, is somebody here?"

A woman's voice called out, "My, you have a beautiful voice. What's your name?"

Out of nowhere, an older woman walked into the light, her eyes riveted on me. I had no idea what she was doing in the park at that late hour or what she wanted from me. I turned and ran home as fast as my legs could run. At an early age I recognized that I was a free spirit who needed to live life my own way, if for no other reason than I simply didn't like being told what to do.

Having modeled myself after my mother, I was often looking for ways to earn money outside the house. As young as six years old, I'd borrow my mother's broom and rake and clean up the neighbors' front yards without permission. When they would ask

Above (on left): Senator Joseph McCarthy (at microphone) launches communist witch hunt. Below: Radio Free Europe.

Don't let her grow up without hearing the TRUTH!

Radio Free Europe

Now! You can broadcast your ideas on Truth and Freedom behind the Iron Curtain over
RADIO FREE EUROPE!

Polish family gathered around radio listening to Radio Free Europe.

what I was doing, I'd point to my work and announce with a smile, "Doesn't it look better?"

Although most would agree, some would run me off with a stern warning to not trespass in their yard again, while others would praise me for being so resourceful and even sometimes reward me with money. After I had saved up enough money, I bought my sisters pretty beads and washed their hair with perfumed shampoo, then with their beautiful beads and shiny hair, I'd take them for a walk down in their newly-washed and ironed dresses down the main street in Bialystok. I was proud of my sisters and looked forward to making their lives better in any way possible, which gave me a strong sense of purpose and value.

I absolutely adored my maternal grandparents, particularly my grandmother Emily who had given birth to three boys and two girls and never had a job outside the family home. Instead, she was the family matriarch who made sure that everything was in working order and that everything and everyone ran on time. Emily was a tall woman, who stood a couple inches shy of six feet, with a beautiful face and her hair pulled back in a bun or tight braid. Like my mother, my grandmother Emily was constantly cooking and cleaning. Her husband, my grandfather Bruno, was a highly successful businessman who was constantly making money, even when he was talking. Beginning when I was young, he began coaching me about practically everything in life.

My grandmother was the one who schooled me on the importance of church. Until World War II, Poland was a religiously diverse society. In the Second Polish Republic, Roman Catholic was the dominant religion, declared by about 65 percent of the Polish citizens that included my family. As a result of the Holocaust and the post–World War II flight and expulsion of German and Ukrainian populations, however, Poland became overwhelmingly Roman Catholic, with nearly 90 percent of the population belonging to the Catholic Church.

Grandma Emily had a beautiful voice, and every morning

she'd sing religious songs, praising and thanking God for all her blessings. To this day I can remember singing "Beautiful Day" and praying beside her on my knees before a holy picture of Jesus. After praying regular prayers from my heart, I prayed prayers from my prayer book. Of course, like all good Catholics, I had a rosary.

On a regular basis my grandmother reminded me that God is everywhere and that throughout my life he would always be watching me. Her message was that when I was a good girl, I'd have good fortune and whenever I considered doing something wrong, God would be watching and I'd have bad fortune. This, of course, was the old teaching of the Catholic Church—this vale of tears and the Old Testament God of Abraham who was a vengeful God to be feared. Thankfully, throughout my childhood, my mother's positive, uplifting outlook on life served to balance the older Catholic Church's negative view of existence.

Because my grandmother put the fear of God in me that led to my believing that God would punish me whenever I was bad, beginning at an early age I became fearful that I'd lose my mother and would sometimes cry and say to her, "Mommy, promise me you're never going to die." I was so attached to her that throughout my childhood the worst times I experienced were when she was sick. In the hope of easing my fear, she'd assure me there was nothing to worry about and then would comfort me by telling me stories she made up on the spot that had a happy ending. That she would do this when she was feeling terribly sick so that I would be comforted is a testament to her unselfish, loving nature.

For most of his life, my father rarely attended church. He wasn't an atheist, but just ignorant about God and religion. This wasn't to say that he wasn't prone to an occasional religious awakening. One such time occurred when my younger sister Alicja was born and my mother informed my father of her intention to baptize Alicja in the Catholic Church. When my father flatly rejected my mother's wish, she cried for days. Then one night she awoke and said to my father, "Listen, I'm very serious. I just saw the devil standing right behind your head and looking down at you."

According to my mother, my father turned white as a sheet. "What are you talking about?" he pleaded.

"I'm not making this up," she continued. "You're going to hell because you don't believe in God."

She must have been convincing because a short while later my father arranged for Alicja to be baptized in the church—at midnight in secret.

Because both my mother and my grandmother Emily were devout Catholics, every Sunday I attended the nine o'clock morning mass, which was for children, regardless of what season it was or the weather condition. Because much of the mass was in Latin, I didn't understand most of the service, although I was captivated by the strikingly beautiful pictures, lights, and candles—and was lulled by the church organ and the choir.

I'm ashamed to admit that my father was a communist. Because of his pampered upbringing, he leaned toward communism because he was looking for an easy road and shortcuts in life, which communism provided him.

After my father graduated from college where he majored in economics, the communists put him in charge of a Walmart-type store that was frequented only by communists, and specifically those in high positions. These stores provided food, clothing, and a wide variety of household goods to the communist elite. The common person couldn't enter these stores, not even to browse.

The communists paid my father a meager salary, which they claimed was supplemented with the prestige he received from managing these stores. An additional part of his compensation was that the communists provided him with a house. Over the years he was relocated to various stores, which was why we lived in many houses. Had it not been for my mother's hard work and

RIGHT: World News – Russians launch first space satellite. BELOW: Liftoff of Russian satellite "Sputnik."

her being the main breadwinner, our family could not have survived solely on my father's salary.

Unfortunately, my father was naïve and oblivious to widespread pilfering being done by the employees. When the communists conducted their annual audit and discovered a sizeable amount of missing merchandise, they blamed my father. Even though he was innocent and hadn't stolen so much as a piece of chocolate for me, this didn't matter to the communists.

When my father first went to work for the communists, he was the perfect model of a communist because he was willing to have the Soviet Union provided his every need for the simple reason that he was a communist. This notion that the communists would provide him with a simple and secure life backfired. As it turned out, instead of being handed an easy life, what he got was eight months in prison.

My mother and I went every day and stood outside the building where my father was incarcerated. She pointed to the small window that was part of his cell. For eight months, I went every day to church and prayed to Saint Jude to help my father come home. One afternoon a priest asked why I was coming every day and praying so hard. When I told him what had happened to my father, the priest said he would pray for him. When my father finally returned home, I took him to the altar where I had prayed incessantly for his release. This was one of the rare, truly sincere moments we ever shared together, and I believe it started him thinking about religion and the power of prayer. Because of his imprisonment and the way my father felt he had been wrongly treated, he lost his job working for the communists and opened a tailor shop in Warsaw.

As an adolescent, I never felt comfortable around communists because ever since they began to occupy Poland, most Polish citizens became paranoid about talking to anyone. Even discussions between father and son couldn't include saying anything against communism for fear that one of them would go to the police and report the other. It seemed that a month didn't pass that there wasn't rumor of someone being locked up for a long period of time because they had spoken out against communism.

With rare exception, my grandmother got her way with me. When I was four years old, I didn't like to shower because I felt it was a waste of time. My grandmother never punished or yelled at me, but would quietly ask if I had washed my face and hands. When I lied and told her I had, she'd say that I missed a spot and would walk me to the bathroom. After washing my face, she'd reel backwards and gasp, "Oh my God, look how beautiful you are! Do you want to see yourself in the mirror?"

Surprised by her revelation, I'd reply, "Really? I'm beautiful?"

"Oh, of course!" she'd continue. "Look at those eyes! And those beautiful ears!"

Because of her attention and compliments, I was transformed from a little girl who didn't care how I looked to a young girl who placed a high importance on being clean, manicured, and well dressed—and believed that one's physical appearance often has much to do with first impressions and is a statement of one's self-image.

In 1953 when I was nine, I overheard my father and several of his communist friends talking negatively about the United States. In my mind, something told me that because the communists had such bad things to say about the United States, it must be a good place. Of course, this tied in with much of what I heard over the years when eavesdropping on the Radio Free Europe broadcasts that repeatedly emphasized that everyone was welcome to come to America. Overcome with a sudden urge to travel to what was being heralded as "The Land of the Free" and "The Land of Op- portunity," I decided to make a trial run.

Having discovered an old rowboat tied to a small pier at one of the lakes, I convinced my five-year-old sister Halina and one of her friends to travel with me by boat to America, which as far as I was concerned was "just around the bend." Early one morning, we snuck away from our homes and commandeered the weath- ered row boat, climbed in, and headed out onto the vast lake,

Above: Soviets parade military might in Red Square. Below: Soviet missiles with atomic warheads.

figuring it would eventually lead to the sea where signs would point to America.

About 20 minutes into our ill-planned sojourn, the boat began to slowly take on water. While my little sister and her friend bailed water with their cupped hands, I jumped from the boat, latched onto the side, and began kicking my feet, hoping to steer it back to shore. When it was clear that our efforts were producing only minimal results, we all began screaming for help.

Fortunately for us, a priest and an altar boy who were coming from morning mass heard our frantic calls and came to our rescue. Ten minutes later, I stood (along with my sister and her friend) soaking wet looking up at the priest who asked in a stern voice, "Where do you live?"

I started crying. "Please! I promise I won't do this again! My father will kill me if he finds out! Haven't you seen me in church?"

The priest studied my face. "Yes, I think so."

"Yes, yes. That was me."

The priest continued to study me for a long while, and then finally said, "All right. You promise you won't do this again. And remember God is going to punish you if you don't keep your promise." He followed this with a hard swat on my behind, which left a mark for two days.

It's a good thing we didn't make it onto the open seas because in January 1954 the United States launched its first atomic submarine *Nautilus*. Three months later, the Soviet Union granted sovereignty to East Germany as US President Dwight Eisenhower set in motion a world atomic pool that purposely excluded the Soviet Union. Tempers were heating up among world leaders, and many people in Poland feared the loudening sound of war drums.

Rising tensions between the United States and the Soviet Union spilled over into Poland when in June of 1957, as I entered my teenage years, a workers' uprising against communist rule in Poznan, Poland was so severely crushed by the communist military that it triggered a violent student protest against communism in neighboring Budapest, Hungary.

If there was trouble here on Earth, it quickly began to spread into space when in October the Soviets launched *Sputnik I*, the first Earth-orbiting satellite, thus triggering the Space Race. In response, in January 1958, Army's Jupiter-C rocket fired the first U.S. Earth satellite, *Explorer I*, into orbit. Amid the growing fear that this Cold War would trigger a hot war and that would launch intercontinental ballistic missiles aimed at Poland, I tried my best to remain positive.

The most exciting times for me as a child were the holidays because I got to help my mother cook for a week and give the house a thorough cleaning from the attic to the basement. In addition, we always got new shoes and clothes for each holiday, like a colorful hat for Easter.

Holidays were a wonderful time to celebrate life for families throughout Poland. The best holiday was Christmas because of Poland's pristine winters. From morning to night, all I could think about was snow, skiing, and ice skating. I'd become so absorbed that I could hardly sleep. When snow was in the forecast, I'd sit by the window, looking up at the sky and at the ground waiting for the first sign of snowflakes. The coldest part of Poland is where we lived in Bialystok where winter was as cold as the Russian Siberian winters, but this never bothered me.

CHAPTER THREE

FIRST LOVE

Francis Gary Powers.

By the spring of 1960, the world was again becoming a dangerous place when US Air Force pilot Francis Gary Powers' U-2 spy plane was shot down over the Soviet Union. Because Powers was unable to activate the plane's self-destruct mechanism before he bailed out, the communists were able to capture Powers when he fell onto Soviet soil, as well as seize the remnants of the spy plane when it fell to Earth. Although the US claimed that the plane was a weather reconnaissance aircraft that had inadvertently wandered off course, the Soviets were convinced they were being spied upon. Within days, a furious Nikita Khrushchev killed the Paris summit conference because of the U-2 incident.

In school, I was told that the Soviets were our friends—the implication being that we shouldn't be afraid of our friends—and that the Soviet military would protect us against any country that invaded Poland. From time to time, I heard my parents discussing the communists. Although my father was in favor of communism, my mother's view of communism was not as favorable. In the 1950s and 1960s, a person who spoke out against the Soviet Union, even subtly, could end up dying in suspicious car accident the next day.

During my earlier adolescence, I had little interest in boys. Unlike the majority of my female school friends, my main interest was sports competition. During school recess, lunchtime, and after school, most of my girlfriends were obsessed with talking about boys. I thought they were crazy and felt sorry for their tortured souls. It wasn't that I hated boys. They were okay, and I did appreciate the company of good boys. Looking back, I'm convinced that I was afraid of the opposite sex because one afternoon I snuck into a movie theater and saw a priest kissing his maid who later became pregnant amid a horrible church/sex scandal. Believing that her tragic condition was due to her kissing that priest, from that moment on, I pushed boys away.

There was one exception—a young boy named Andrew Krywczenko who lived next door when I was nine years old. He was somewhat frail, which made him appear harmless. Within a month, however, he started destroying my toys. It wasn't long before I hated the sight of him and would call him names and take off running. After a while, he lost interest in me, then in middle school I ran into him again. My hair was long, and he'd sneak up behind me and yank on it. In the classroom and during recess, he'd try to trip me whenever no one was looking. Thank God my family moved to another neighborhood, and I felt relieved that I'd finally seen the last of him.

A few years later, I was enrolled in high school where, as a freshman, I appeared in the school play in the leading role of a clown. My performance came off so well that I became the talk of the school. Even my drama teacher commented that I should be in movies because I had a natural acting talent.

In my newfound notoriety, I became friends with one of the more popular girls. One Friday night we attended a school dance that was held at the boy's gymnasium. Although I didn't know how to dance, I loved listening to the music. A half hour into the evening, my girlfriend pointed to a boy who was headed our way, commenting that he was a great dancer. One look at this boy and I shrieked.

"What's wrong?" my girlfriend asked as she took hold of my arm, thinking I might faint.

"He used to be my terrible neighbor Andrew!"

As it turned out, Andrew had moved away for two years and had recently returned to Bialystok and become *her* boyfriend. They had broken up, and she thought he intended on asking her to dance. To my amazement—if not horror—he walked past her without so much as a glance in her direction and asked me to dance. I was speechless, which wasn't like me. Not only did I not know how to dance, but— *it was him!*

After a few moments, I managed to compose myself. It was then that I noticed that Andrew had become a handsome young boy with an athletic build. Not wanting to embarrass myself on the dance floor, I talked my way out of the dance and spent the rest of the evening staying close to a group of girls and avoiding his glances.

In the weeks that followed, I became determined to learn how to dance and began practicing at home. I wasn't teaching myself to dance because I wanted the boys to like me. Dancing had become a challenging sports endeavor, and within a short time I became good. Soon the boys in school noticed my dancing ability, especially Andrew.

At the time I became reacquainted with Andrew, I was un-aware that he had a physical disability, which was easy to miss because he was so strong looking. Because he was such a fine dancer and immaculate dresser, many of the girls would look out the windows whenever he walked down the street. Because of his popularity, there were times when groups of jealous neighbor-hood boys wanted to beat him up. Although Andrew was game, and I was confident he would prevail in a fight, I would pull him away and tell those rowdy boys to scram. Besides being attracted to his intelligence, he was no longer the aggressive bratty kid that I recalled years ago and had become refreshingly nonthreatening.

According to Andrew, he liked me because I was in sports, full of energy, and always in a good mood. Although Andrew looked athletic, he didn't compete in sports because, according to him, because of his physical disability, which he chose not to discuss, and I didn't pry.

Over the next several years, we'd meet at remote places, mainly recreational parks and lakes, and now and then taking in a movie. The reason we were sneaking around was because my parents didn't want me to date and, more importantly, they had already found a rich architect whom they were determined I would marry once I turned of age. This architect was slightly older than I was and well established, even having a village named after him. Not surprisingly, my parents were shocked when I told them I wasn't interested and instead had other plans.

In the early 1960s, the determinations of the United States and the Soviet Union to dominate the world continued to escalate when in April 1961, Soviet pilot and cosmonaut Yuri Alekseyevich Gagarin became the first human to journey into outer space when his spacecraft completed an orbit of Earth. At the close of 1961, Soviet Premier Nikita Khrushchev banged his shoe on the desk at a meeting of the United Nations General Assembly, proclaiming, "We will bury you!"

The landmark feat in space by the Soviets, coupled with Khrushchev's bold proclamation, put pressure on the United States. Two months later, the United States answered the challenge as Lt. Col. John H. Glenn, Jr. became the first American to orbit Earth.

In 1962 at the age of 18, I graduated from the Technology of Design, with plans of finding work in the garment industry as a fabric designer. A short while later, my plans of becoming a clothing designer were sidelined when I decided to attend law college that was located 130 miles away in Lubin.

Although my mother had for years impressed upon me that if I wanted to live a comfortable life, I needed to be accomplished in something, my father was anything but supportive. As far as he

Nikita Khrushchev 1960.

was concerned, I was a girl and should focus on learning how to cook and making myself as pretty as possible so that I could land a well-to-do husband. In his mind, this was in line with what the communists foresaw as the future of most women.

I said to my father, "What do you mean by *most* women? Are you saying that not all communist women are destined to be homemakers?"

After a brief silence, he shrugged. "Well, I suppose so."

"Good," I continued. "From what you say, the communists once helped you, so maybe communism will help me. I'm going to look into it and become the best communist in Poland." He seemed to like the sound of that. It wasn't that long ago that he had been disgraced and thrown in jail. Perhaps now I could rehabilitate his good standing.

A month later, I enrolled in a college class on communism, determined to become a big star among its ranks. Once again my parents would be welcomed into those special stores that my father once managed—the ones for the elite communists. In no time, we were all going to be living back in favor.

After the first week of class, however, it was clear that I wasn't destined to become a big shot in Poland's communist regime and was shown the door. The problem was that I asked too many questions about which the instructor either didn't have answers or had answers he knew the students—and even worse, the communists—wouldn't like.

Over time I found that the more I learned about communism, the more stupid it sounded. The most glaring problem was that its system worked against the individual whose dreams weren't in agreement with the basic principles of communism. Although communism looked good on paper, in reality, it amounted to a lot of unfulfilled promises. Worst of all, communism went against my strong competitive nature and my belief that, when it came to my future, the sky was the limit. As I had learned from my mother, I was willing to work hard for the things I wanted in life—not only for myself, but for my family. I had no interest in working day and night to improve myself and my living condition so that I can give money to people in the Soviet Union who sat on barstools all day drinking vodka. Besides placing limits on my dreams and my financial future, communism wouldn't allow me to travel to and from Poland of my own free will or to attend church. Now that it was clear to everyone that a career in communist politics wasn't for me, I soon left home to pursue my law studies in Lubin where I lived in a college dorm.

To my surprise and delight, upon entering college, the portal of knowledge of world news opened and, as a result, I became increasingly aware of the Cold War between the Soviet Union and the United States.

Terrifyingly, worsening relations between the two superpowers came to a head when on October 22, 1962, after reviewing photographic evidence, President John F. Kennedy informed the world that the Soviet Union was building secret missile bases in Cuba, just 90 miles off the shores of Florida. For the next 13 days, the world held its breath as the Soviet Union and the United States confronted each other about missiles stationed in Cuba.

US warship threatens Soviet freighter carrying missiles to Cuba.

US blockade of Cuba newspaper headlines.

Meanwhile in America, Senator Joseph McCarthy's escalated witch hunt for communist sympathizers, persons guilty of un-American activities, and downright spies residing in the United States contributed to the growing dissension between the two superpowers.

Then in August 1962, the East Germans erected the Berlin Wall between East and West Berlin. A year later the USSR detonated a 50-megaton hydrogen bomb, which was to date the biggest explosion in history. As the threat of all-out nuclear war continuing to rise, a Washington-to-Moscow "hot line" communications link was opened, which was designed to reduce risk of accidental war. One month later on November 22, 1963, President John F. Kennedy was assassinated in Dallas.

In February 1965, a month before my 21st birthday, I returned to Bialystok during my college winter break. Andrew was overjoyed to see me, and over the next six weeks we spent consid-

1962 Berlin Wall.

erable time together. He had matured considerably. He had more self-confidence, and I was impressed by his overall common sense and practical approach to life.

I guess he must have felt the same about me because a few days before I was to return to college, during the intermission of a movie we had gone to see, he told me that he was afraid that someone at my college in Lubin was going to steal me away and asked me to marry him. Because my father was a terrible husband, and my mother always told me, you can have five or ten kids, but you have only one husband—and he's the most important person in your life—I promised myself I'd never marry out of fear that I'd marry someone like my father.

On the other hand, this was the mid-1960s when upon graduating high school the majority of girls married and began having children. Being honest with myself, I knew that I had been dreaming for some time about having a child. Like so many other young women, I wanted a baby like a little doll. Of course, if I were married to Andrew, I would be responsible for taking care of him and our house, so it would be good to have a baby. Most important of all, Andrew had unofficially been my boyfriend for several years and had many great qualities. Early in our friendship, he shared with me that his mother hadn't taken good care of him and after his biological father was killed in WWII, his mother married a man who didn't like Andrew. So in a way, I felt compassion for him and, now that we had grown closer, wanted to take care of him.

In addition, I wanted to please my parents, especially my mother and grandmother, who were extremely family oriented and wanted grandchildren. And so after giving Andrew's proposal thought, I accepted. Because we had little money, and even less time, there was no formal wedding ceremony. Besides not having photos and a cake, we didn't even have wedding bands.

At that time, Andrew was living with his mother and stepfather, and I had been staying with my parents during my semester break. Having agreed that honeymooning at my mother's house

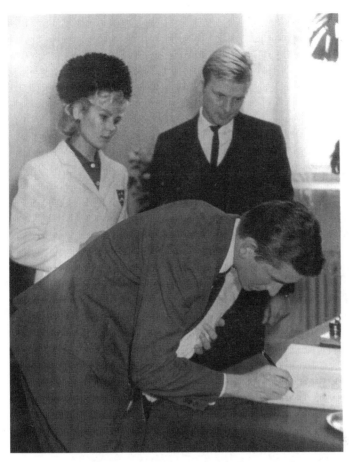

Andrew and I on our formal wedding day.

was better than staying with Andrew's parents, we snuck into my bedroom late that night. The next morning, my mother knocked on my door to invite me to breakfast. Hearing no response, she opened the door, and when she saw a man in my bed, she shrieked.

"Momma, wait!" I yelled before she flew into a rage. "This is my husband!"

She stood in silent shock for several moments, then broke down in tears and ran to tell my father, who immediately launched World War III. For the next several minutes, he called me a stupid idiot, followed by a barrage of insults. When he paused to catch his breath, I asked him if he could think of any more words in the

Top: My sister Alicja on her wedding-day. BELOW: Farny Church in Bialystok where I was married.

dictionary to hurt me. When the dust finally settled, my parents could not undo what was obvious—Andrew and I were married. The earthshaking problem now, according to my mother, was that the marriage hadn't taken place in the Catholic Church in front of a priest. As such, the marriage wasn't legal in the eyes of the Church, which meant that I was living in sin.

Adamant and determined that the marriage be sanctified by the Church, my mother arranged for a wedding before a priest and 200 people to witness our marriage ceremony, which was followed by a gala reception. After several hours of everyone joyously drinking, eating, and dancing, Andrew turned to me and said, "Let's go to a movie." I told him that we couldn't leave because we were the most important people there. Having convinced me that no one would miss us, he took me to the movie theater where he had proposed marriage a month earlier. When the movie ended, we returned to the reception; I donned my wedding dress, and we strolled back into the reception hall where it was clear that few guests had missed us.

Although Andrew was previously reluctant to talk about his physical disability, now that we were married, he recognized that I needed to discuss this with him. After all, I was now his wife and was taking our marriage seriously. In plain and simple terms, Andrew's disability was that since childhood he had a malfunctioning heart valve that needed to be surgically repaired. Of course, an operation of this nature was going to cost a considerable amount of money.

Andrew had been on government disability for many years. A company that hired disabled people had hired him to manage a food store. In addition, he subsidized his income by selling a popular line of clothing that he designed.

Realizing that it would take years for me to graduate from college and that I needed to focus my attention on getting my

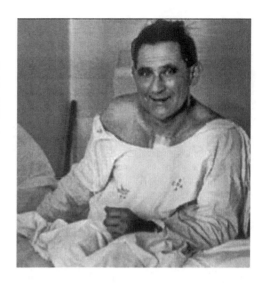

RIGHT: Louis Washkansky, first heart transplant. OPPOSITE: Standard M-20 Warszawa.

husband well, I dropped out of school. Pulling on the optimism I had learned from my mother, I began researching our options. Although in the mid-1960s there were no heart surgeons in Poland, I learned about the first human heart transplant that was performed in December 1967 in Johannesburg, South Africa by Dr. Christian Barnard and a team of South African surgeons. The patient was a 54-year-old grocer who suffered from diabetes and incurable heart disease. Although the patient survived the complex operation, he died 18 days later. I became determined to find a way to have Andrew operated on. There simply was no choice. Without this operation, he would gradually become an invalid and die at an early age, which I wasn't going to allow to happen. My husband was going to be okay. All we needed to do was earn more money.

While Andrew and I were living at my mother's home, I became pregnant and gave birth on December 18, 1966 to our beautiful, healthy daughter whom we named Jolanta. We had been wishing for child for a long time, and so Jolanta was the answer to our prayers.

Because she was born eight weeks premature, I stayed in the hospital in Bialystok for several weeks before the doctors allowed me to take her home. From the moment Andrew laid eyes on our

newborn daughter, she became a top priority. Because the doctors told me that I would be breastfeeding her for several months and that it was vital that my breast milk be highly nourishing, Andrew traveled to Budapest, Hungary to purchase several months' supply of a special food for me.

One afternoon when I was in the hospital with Jolanta, Andrew came to visit and told me that he had bought a car for me—a Warszawa M-20, which was Poland's version of the German Volkswagen "people's car." While owning a car wouldn't have been a big deal for many young people living in the United States, in the mid-1960s a private Polish citizen owning a car in Poland was extremely rare. This was because only the communists owned new cars, and those few Polish citizens who owned used cars purchased them at a highly inflated price at auctions or from private parties. With few exceptions, as was the case with the car Andrew purchased, these used cars were in serious need of engine and cosmetic repair, and many turned out to be beyond repair.

He worked tirelessly for months on that car, and he was finished, the car looked and ran like it was brand new. I was truly proud of him, as well as impressed with his persistence and dedication to set a goal and see it through to its completion. His tenacity reminded me of my mother, who often told me that I should never start any job unless I'm willing to see it through to perfection. I know that she was as proud of Andrew's pristine reconditioning of that car as I was.

After returning to my parents' home, life became uncomfortable. As is often the case with new grandmothers, my mother immediately began fussing over Jolanta and often criticized how I was taking care of my baby. In my mother's eyes, I couldn't do anything right. Besides not knowing how to properly breastfeed Jolanta, my mother felt that I didn't know how to dress her, bed her down, or even change her diapers. Although my mother's fretting made life better for baby Jolanta, her constant meddling made life miserable for me. I wanted to enjoy my baby, and my mother, although well meaning, made that difficult if not impossible. In addition, my parents began to make negative comments about Andrew. Because they didn't know about his heart condition, they felt he was lazy because he wouldn't help move furniture and at times walked slowly. With our situation rapidly deteriorating, my mother said it would be better for everyone if we found our own place.

Two days later, we moved into the apartment of Andrew's parents. From the start I didn't feel comfortable because it was obvious that Andrew's mother didn't like me. In my view, she was the type of mother who wouldn't welcome any woman into the family. To her, no woman was ever good enough for her son.

That my husband and I, along with our newborn, were sharing a small bedroom made matters worse. After a month, it became necessary to hire a part-time babysitter because I was having episodes of heart arrhythmia, which the doctors thought was caused by my going from being highly active in sports for many years to suddenly leading a sedentary life—or stress. I knew my arrhythmia was being caused by the latter. For many reasons, and probably more on the horizon, it was clear to me that Andrew and I needed our own apartment. There was a major problem, however.

The year was 1968 and I was 24 years of age. Unlike the housing in the United States and other free societies throughout the world at that time, in Poland one didn't simply go out and rent an apartment from a private property owner. Instead, the only way anyone obtained an apartment was to submit an application to the government. Because the wait time to get an apartment was between 15 and 30 years, I needed to find a way to drastically speed up the process. I wasn't 100 percent confident, nor did I have any proof, but I suspected that many individuals obtained apartments quickly by passing money under the table to the right person—and I decided to gamble.

I wrote a letter to the government housing department and requested an explanation about why certain people were getting apartments much faster than others and thus avoiding the long wait period. I wrote, "I have arrhythmia and my husband has a heart problem. We live on the fourth floor of his parents' apartment that isn't equipped with an elevator, and his parents are very unfriendly towards us." Moreover, I mentioned that I had the names of these special people who received express apartments, and although I realized I wasn't going to get my apartment as quickly as they did, I wanted to know when this was going to happen.

Two days later, a man called from the housing department and requested that I come to his office to discuss my letter. The following morning when I arrived, he wasted no time getting down to business.

"I read your letter and would like to know what you know," he began.

He drew heavily on his cigarette, then blew the smoke upwards into his unkempt hair. I could tell from his jaundiced eyes that he was a heavy drinker.

"Everything I wrote in my letter is true," I replied. "What else is there to know?"

ABOVE: Following 1968 TET Offensive, civilians sort through the ruins of their homes in Cholon, the heavily damaged Chinese section of Saigon. BELOW: Vietnam, US Huey choppers support US ground troops.

"Can you give me the names you mentioned?" he said. "I'd like to look into this."

I didn't have any names. "Do you think I'm stupid?" I said.

"You know those names, and I know those names. You think I'm suicidal? I must know something because if I don't, I'd be in jail."

The man squirmed in his chair and then glanced out his window. I sensed that he was worried because his taking money under the table could get him fired and even thrown in prison. He turned back to me, his forehead now glistening with perspiration. "Would you like some coffee?" he said nervously. "Cigarette?"

"This isn't a friendly party," I said bluntly. "This is business. What I want is my apartment."

After a long, uncomfortable silence, he spoke slowly, carefully choosing his words. "What do you say if I tell you you're going to get your apartment this year?"

"I say I deserve it. And I already know the exact apartment I want."

"Oh?" he said with a raised brow. "And what apartment is that?"

When I gave him the exact location of the apartment, which was on a second floor and had several choice amenities, he objected. "I gave this apartment already to someone else."

"This is not my problem," I countered. "This is your problem."

He glared at me for a long while, then smiled weakly, exposing his chipped teeth. "All right then. You're going to get that apartment this year."

Twenty minutes later I practically danced into our food store and told Andrew about my meeting. Earlier, after reading my accusatory letter, Andrew warned me not to send it.

"You're joking," he said nervously.

"I'm not joking. I'm just coming from a meeting at the housing department. Our meeting was a simple business matter."

"Well, congratulations," he said with a sigh. "Jolanta and I will visit you in jail."

Two weeks later we moved into our new apartment that was located across the street from my parents' home. The apartment had two bedrooms, a bathroom, a nice airy kitchen, and a pleasant view. So that there would be no hard feelings, Andrew and I took this kind man from the housing department to dinner, being sure that we met at a discreet location outside Bialystok. It was a festive evening that culminated with that generous and understanding government official getting deliriously drunk and showering me with kisses on my cheek and repeatedly shaking Andrew's hand.

As the 1960s came to an end, hostile relations between the United States and Soviet Union continued to intensify, and I became increasingly concerned that their hostilities would eventually would spill over into Poland. Of course, the worst hotspot in the world was Vietnam where the communists launched the Tet Offensive that resulted in giving them the upper hand. In response, US troops began invading Cambodia. It seemed that Vietnam had become a wasteland of blood and the scattered body parts of men, women, and even children. I began to worry just how far the leaders of these two superpowers were willing to take things.

Around that same timeframe, political and religious leaders were being killed in the United States, including Martin Luther King, Jr. and Senator Robert Kennedy, while on the opposite side of the world Czechoslovakia was invaded by the Soviet and Warsaw Pact forces. If there was a bright side, it occurred on July 20, 1969 when *Apollo II* landed on the moon and astronauts Neil Armstrong, Edwin Aldrin, and Michael Collins became the first humans to walk on the lunar surface. Maybe, just maybe, there was still hope for a peaceful world.

July 1969 Moon landing.

CHAPTER FOUR

CHICKEN FARM

Thankfully, over the next year things ran smoothly. Andrew worked at our government-owned deli while I settled into being a mother and homemaker. Our daughter Jolanta, who was now four years old, was doing well and was in great spirits and a joy to be around.

When Andrew and I realized we weren't making much headway with saving money for his heart surgery, he suggested that we go into the chicken farming business, which was a far cry from any business venture I would have envisioned. My first choice would have been to invest in a classy boutique that catered to women. Given Andrew's experience in designing clothing and my background in fabric, a women's clothing boutique would have been a natural. Surely a chicken farm didn't interest me in the least. Nevertheless, because I knew that my husband was a good businessperson with keen foresight, I agreed to his proposition. If necessary, my mother could help care for Jolanta if I were needed to work the farm.

The first step in putting together the chicken farm was to lease a parcel of land, which we were able to acquire. The land was a 15-minute drive from our apartment. Next was to obtain a government bank loan in the form of a line of credit, which we'd need for constructing the building that would house the chickens and our initial purchase of day-old chick hatchlings. After we deposited money that we borrowed from friends and family into our bank, the government agreed to fund our farm.

The business deal was basic. Our company would be government owned and our salaries would be paid by monthly draws

Also special chickens, white meat only, with sister's husband Bogdon.

from our line of credit. The majority of our chickens would be sent to the Soviet Union, and whatever amount, if any, that exceeded their required allotment, could stay in Poland. Andrew and I had nothing to say about this; the Soviet Union was going to be our boss. Our job was to purchase day-old chicks, raise them to full grown, and then ship them wherever the communists told us. Side money might be gained selling chicken manure to local farmers as fertilizer. As long as we kept current with our loan payments, the government would continue to release conservative installments from our line of credit, which we regularly needed to purchase chicken food and hatchlings.

Having obtained our initial funding, we constructed a small building that could house 5,000 chickens. We essentially did all the work ourselves.

In order to assure their best chance of survival, the temperature in the chicken house had to be kept at 90 degrees Fahrenheit. Because we initially didn't have a central heating system, we planned to purchase a coal-burning stove, which we felt would generate enough heat for our start-up order of 500 chicks. Besides keeping the temperature at 90 degrees Fahrenheit, it was vital that the temperature not drop more than a half degree per hour. Keeping these chicks warm was critical, especially during their first three weeks of life. After that, they were strong enough to tolerate bigger climate changes.

I purchased day-old chicks from a nearby hatchery that sold hens and eggs, but no roosters. I'd arrive at the hatchery in a truck and transport the chicks back to our farm.

When the chicks reached their full adult size in eight weeks, I put them back on the truck and drove them to the slaughterhouse. It was next to impossible to not fall in love with these baby chicks. I loved the fresh smell of baby chicks first thing in the morning. They seemed so cheerful and eager to play. The baby roosters with their little red bonnet were the cutest to watch when they'd try to fight with each other. The fact that there were hundreds of them darting around at one time, and they all pretty much looked alike, thankfully prevented me from getting attached to any one of them.

The first time I drove chickens to the slaughterhouse was a terrible experience. I went behind the slaughterhouse and cried for hours. After that, I had to approach those deliveries as being strictly business. I needed to make those deliveries without a heart. It was the only way I could get through them emotionally.

Conducting business with the communists was never easy. There was always someone, somewhere along the chain, who demanded something that was outside the guidelines of fair business. Acquiring a stove was one such example.

In Poland during those years, any social party, even a small gathering of neighbors, included the drinking of alcohol, which the communists allowed its citizens to manufacture. Although the

Polish version of American moonshine was against the law, the communists overlooked its manufacture. Among most Poles, and especially Poles who sympathized with the communists, anyone who didn't drink alcohol was either sick or considered unfriendly. Because of this, the inclusion of liquor in most business deals was a standard practice.

An older friend who had for years done business with the communists gave me a piece of advice. "When you go to that store to negotiate buying that stove, wear some nice makeup and a sexy dress."

"To buy a stove?" I replied, insulted.

"Yes. And be sure to keep your wits about you."

A week later I arrived at the communist-run store to purchase the coal-burning stove and brought a gift in the form of a bottle of Courvoisier cognac.

I was greeted by a man named Janek. He was bald, 30 pounds overweight, and had hair growing from his nostrils and ears. His beady eyes gave me the once over, then he smiled as he accepted the bottle of cognac. "All right, nice to see you. I can accept this gift on one condition—we drink it together."

I wanted to break the bottle over his shiny head, but remembered that my friend told me to keep my wits about me. "I'm not an Italian streetwalker," I replied with a patronizing smile. "I'm a businesswoman. The cognac is my way of saying thank you for helping me buy a stove for a fair price. Without a stove, my chickens will die and I'll lose a lot of money."

His eyes twinkled. "I see. Of course," he said. "Please sit down. My name is Janek. Can I call you Jolanta?"

"Sure," I replied.

"So what kind of stove do you want?"

I described the stove in detail, although it was clear that he was paying little attention. When I finished, he said, "How long are you staying in Siedlce?"

"A few days. I want to look around."

"Okay. Can we have dinner tonight?"

The thought sent a chill up my spine. I quickly regained my composure. "Of course, but I'll pay for my—"

"No, ladies don't pay when I invite them," he said with finality. "What hotel are you staying at?"

I told him I hadn't yet found a hotel and asked which one he recommended. He recommended the best hotel in Siedlce, and an hour later I checked in. At Janek's request, I called to inform him what room I was in and asked what he'd like after dinner to drink. He was delighted to have received my call and elated over my offer of more liquor.

"Boizel champagne."

"Wonderful."

He hung up and called back in 30 minutes to check if I was actually at the hotel and staying in that room number. He was thrilled that I hadn't given him misinformation. "You know, Jolanta, I have a gift for you."

Outside the chicken farm.

"Really? How nice," I replied cheerfully. "What gift?"

"The stove. I already sent it to your farm in Bialystok for free."

"Oh, how thoughtful."

"Yes, of course," he agreed. "I will come to the hotel in one hour to pick you up we will have a splendid evening together." This was followed by what sounded like slobbering.

"Of course. I'll be in the hotel lobby in one hour. Goodbye."

I hung up the phone and cringed. It was all I could do to stop from screaming. Quickly gathering my things, I packed and departed the hotel within 45 minutes, having left Janek a note telling him I was sorry that I couldn't keep our dinner date, but that I had to return to Bialystok because of an emergency. I thanked him for everything and told him he was a great man and that he would forever be my friend. I left the note at the front desk, along with a case of Boizel champagne that I procured from the hotel's dining room and drove home.

The following morning the phone rang. I wasn't surprised to hear Janek's voice complaining on the other end.

"I'm so sorry, Janek, I really am. I was in such a hurry that I didn't even have time to call you."

"Yes, yes, that's fine," he said impatiently. "And thank you for the champagne—and the cognac, of course—but our agreement was that I would not be drinking it alone." He was suddenly quiet. I could sense his waiting anticipation. After a few moments, I said, "Drink it with your wife." There was another long silence, and then the line went dead.

This was typical of communist corruption infiltrating businesses in Poland and grumblings could be heard among Polish workers and business owners. As the Soviets continued their determination to keep the workers down, there was confidential talk among workers to unionize and form a politically active Worker's Party. At the time, no one knew how potentially catastrophic the forming of this union would become.

With our new stove installed and working efficiently, Andrew and I continued to make improvements on our small chicken house, installing a new floor and upgrading to a central heating system. Everything was moving so smoothly that we built a second chicken house that was twice the size of the first one. Together, the two houses became home to 15,000 chickens. When I walked into either of the chicken houses, the floor looked like it was covered by a huge bright yellow carpet. These thousands of chickens silently running around was a spectacular sight to see.

In June 1972, I learned that I was pregnant, which was great news to Jolanta, who was now age four and desperately wanted a younger brother or sister. Thankfully, Andrew and I would be able to afford a new addition to our family. Together with Andrew's small salary, his sideline clothing business, his monthly disability check, and money from raising chickens, I managed to work an occasional odd job that helped add to our savings account for Andrew's heart surgery.

Then on Christmas Eve of 1972 in the early morning hours tragedy struck. As had occurred with my mother 28 years earlier, I unexpectedly went into premature labor and was rushed to the hospital. As my difficult labor continued, at three o'clock in the morning the EKG monitoring my heart suddenly flatlined. While one team of doctors and nurses struggled to deliver my baby, another team narrowly managed to bring me back to life. Ten minutes later my baby, a boy, was born, but died a short while later in my arms. Around that same time, I learned that my younger sister Halina had died in a tragic car accident 700 miles away in Budapest. Ironically, during that 30 minute timeframe, the three of us—I, my newborn son, and my younger sister Halina—had died. Only I survived.

The hours, days, and weeks that followed were filled with sadness. In addition to my sister Halina's body having to be brought to Poland for burial and funeral services, funeral arrangements needed to be arranged for the burial of my infant son. Thankfully, my son was baptized at the hospital before he died, which meant that he could have a full Christian burial that included the Eucharist.

It took a long time for me to recover emotionally, which I could not have done without my mother. The fact that my mother and I had both lost infant sons was a bond that only two mothers can share. As was the case with many tragedies that I was yet to face in my life, my mother's love and compassion helped get me out of the darkness and back into the light.

With the passing weeks, I worked every day alone in both chicken houses. I didn't have a friend; I didn't go anywhere; I didn't even know what the popular music was anymore. All I had was the farm and home, the farm and home, day after day. I was willing to do this because Andrew and I had nearly saved the full amount of money that was needed for his heart surgery. The dark cloud that hung over me appeared to have a small silver lining, and within time I was back to my old self.

Although Andrew was devastated by the loss of our baby, he recovered more quickly by focusing on his work. Two months after we built the second chicken house, a major company moved next to our deli store that Andrew had continued managing fulltime. This new company had 3,000 workers, and every day at lunchtime the company ordered cold cuts for its employees. Needless to say, Andrew had his hands full. At some point, he became convinced that I had the much easier job. One day he arrived at the farm and told me, "Your vacation is over. You're going to work in the store. I'm going to work here."

"Fine," I said agreeably, smiling to myself.

Maintaining the chicken farm was hard work. Everything had to be constantly cleaned and everyone's clothes and shoes needed to be changed between chicken houses. Moreover, everything and everyone had to be frequently disinfected to protect against a virus that could wipe out the entire chicken population in a matter of days, if not hours. I even purchased a microscope and conducted autopsies on chickens that seemingly died from illness. Then there were the chicks themselves. Those 15,000 chickens ate two tons of chicken food daily. This feed was supplied by carrying two buckets at a time and spreading it throughout the chicken house, the small house being 2,000 square feet, and the bigger house being 4,000 square feet. The labor of distributing chicken feed was minor compared to what was needed to maintain the temperature. Before the installation of central heating, coal had to be carried to the stove, and several times a day its interior had to be cleaned and the ash disposed of—as well as cleaning the walls and floors—and I did all of this by myself, and I weighed all of 110 pounds soaking wet. Put simply, I resembled a big chicken

Early Saturday morning at three a.m., I tapped Andrew on the shoulder and said, "It's time to get up."

"It's summer and it's hot," he said in a groggy voice.

"There's more to our chicken houses than heat," I replied. "You have to drive over there and change the water and feed them and clean up their mess."

With some encouragement, Andrew got out of bed and headed off a half hour later for the farm. I stayed and cared for Jolanta when she awoke, then after she went off to school, joined Andrew.

About an hour into the daily routine, he stopped to rest. "You do this every day?"

"I do this several times a day, seven days a week."

"You must be mad."

With Andrew ready to quit, I told him he wasn't finished.

"What do you mean, not finished?" he said as he wiped a wall of perspiration from his forehead. "You are mentally sick. We could die here in this chicken farm."

"Do you have another choice?" I asked.

He didn't. But being the businessperson that he was—actually now an enlightened one—the following week he arranged to have two people begin helping me because he had every intention of returning to our deli store—permanently.

The truth is that Andrew and I were like a farmer's two-horse pulling team. When hitched in double harness, the key to a pulling a wagon is the two horses need to work together. As they pull the wagon down the road, two horses never pull with the same strength. One is always stronger or more tired than the other, and both horses sense that. As a result, one horse pulls harder, thus allowing its partner to rest. And the two horses continually switch places throughout their journey. Some people think it's the wagon driver jawing and his whip that tells the team how to pull, but this isn't the case. The wagon master simply steers the team and tells them how fast to go and when to stop. Throughout our marriage, Andrew and I were a perfect team, one always taking over when the other tired, then when rested, picking up the load again to allow the other to rest.

Although after Andrew and I married, my mother grew to dislike him, by the time the chicken farm was in full swing, she fell in love with him; and he loved her more than his own mother. Every night before retiring, he walked across the street to see my mother. As it turned out, they had much in common. She respected him and felt that he was a hard worker, as well as a good husband and father. Everyone felt that it was highly commendable that he worked as hard as he did without consideration of his heart condition.

To my dismay, the degree of hard, back-breaking work that I was doing at our chicken farm wasn't necessary. A year after we began our operation, I traveled to Sweden because I wanted to see how its chicken farms were operated. Sweden was also where I was regularly funneling money for Andrew's surgery. I was taken aback. The Swedes' operation was completely automated. Everything was push button and climate controlled. The loss of chickens from disease was practically nil. Because of their far superior operation, their profit margin easily eclipsed ours.

When I returned to Poland, I went straight to the Minister of Agriculture and told him what I'd seen in Sweden, assuring him that I could have 100,000 chickens on my farm and make ten times the money for the communists if he would authorize a minimal increase of my line of credit in order to make improvements. Moreover, I told him I didn't mind paying a high increase in taxes and that when I got rich, the communists would get rich. In fact, I welcomed this high tax increase.

To my disgust, not only was he not interested, he was insulted that I'd even bring up what was going on in Sweden. "Don't tell me what I have to do," he barked, and then looked down at his desk and shuffled paperwork.

I walked out, knowing for certain what I had suspected for many years—that communism was stupid. I wanted much more for my life and the lives of my family. I wanted us to live life to the fullest and to have our biggest dreams come true. Even if they didn't come true, I wanted the right to at least try to make my dreams become reality. Most important of all, I didn't want to live in fear of another communist armed occupation like my mother and father had lived through at the outset of World War II. Although the majority of my energy was focused on getting Andrew to Sweden for his heart surgery, I was growing increasingly concerned over the negative impact the communists were having on my beloved country of Poland.

By winter of 1973, it was clear that Andrew's heart condition was worsening and we could no longer put off his opera-

These are special chickens, one that caused the tax.

tion. We had saved barely enough money to afford the operation and transportation to the hospital in Stockholm, Sweden where the surgery was to be performed by heart surgeon Dr. Milford Cummings.

It had taken months for me to find Dr. Cummings, who loved the Polish people. I was unstoppable. If I was turned away at one place, I looked elsewhere. If I was told no and taken out the door, I came down the chimney. I simply wouldn't take no for an answer.

Prior to the surgery, it was necessary to perform a battery of pre-operative tests that included full dye-imaging of Andrew's heart, as well as measuring the blood pressures in each of the four heart chambers. Because these pre-op procedures would be considerably less expensive if done in Poland, and the results would be accepted by the Swedish surgical team, Andrew and I agreed to have the tests done in Warsaw. This would also mean that Andrew would spend less time in the hospital in Stockholm, which amounted to additional savings.

Unfortunately, we made a wrong—and fatal—decision. Days after the tests were conducted in Poland, Andrew's heart began bleeding and his blood pressure steadily fell. When the bleeding couldn't be stopped and there was no time for an emergency flight to Stockholm, Andrew passed away at the age of 32.

My immediate concern was for our daughter Jolanta, who was six years old when her father died. For two weeks, I'd been returning home and telling Jolanta that her daddy was all right, and now suddenly I had to tell her that he had died, which she didn't understand. God must have been watching over her because she came through the ordeal remarkably well. Perhaps her saving grace were her school friends who rallied around her and brought her flowers. In just a brief time, she became everyone's child, and she liked this. Years later, her recollection of that time in her life was that she "was a hero and everybody liked me."

I was devastated by Andrew's death. Not only had I lost my husband and Jolanta's father, but Andrew and I had worked hard

Andrew's funeral.

for years and saved religiously so that he could have this life-saving operation. Week after week, month after month, we smuggled money to Sweden (the communists did not allow money to be sent out of the country). I even arranged for a private plane to transport Andrew to Sweden. And now he was gone, suddenly and unexpectedly. We had come so close. My hopes of a successful operation in Stockholm couldn't have been higher. I never for one second imagined that Andrew could die from those pretests. And now here I was, along with my family, back at the church and cemetery with yet another funeral.

I suddenly felt like the weight of the world had been placed on my shoulders. Besides a substantial loan on the farm, I was now solely financially responsible for our car loan and 30 more years of paying for our apartment. There was no time to sit and cry and pray—there was only time to roll up my sleeves and work harder.

My mother instilled in me at an early age that when you work hard, God will help; in essence, the old adage "God helps those who help themselves." If I suddenly find myself stranded in a lifeboat in the middle of the ocean, it's perfectly fine to pray, but God expects me to row.

Without Andrew's business acumen, I knew I needed a well-defined plan. I was good at following carefully laid out instructions. I needed to be prepared because I was the only one in charge. I felt that I had to analyze every single aspect. I made a daily hour-by-hour plan that meticulously spelled out what I needed to do from the moment I arrived at the farm in the pre-dawn hours until the moment I left the farm at night. Then in the evening I took my plan and made notes as to what worked and what didn't and how I had to change my approach. I didn't have the liberty to get lost, because if that happened, everything would collapse. There were times when I was scared and couldn't sleep. One night I awoke worried that a virus would wipe out my chickens. I got out of bed, dressed, and then drove to the farm where I scrubbed down both chicken houses with disinfectant. I was awakened the next morning by my workers who found me asleep on the floor beside my pail of disinfectant, a brush still in my hand.

The year was 1973. I suppose that subconsciously I wanted to die from starvation because I literally stopped eating. I was angry with God for taking my husband, as well as my sister Halina and my infant son. My mother said these deaths were part of God's plan to make me stronger. I didn't want to hear it, and I stopped going to church and stopped praying. Although my brain quit working and I was no longer eating, I had a seven-year-old daughter to raise.

Even though I was now a young widow living in a male-driven society, I still had prestige in Poland because there was an escalating food shortage and I ran a chicken farm. Because of this, everywhere I went, people would smile and comment, "Good morning, Mrs. Jolanta." "Good evening, Mrs. Jolanta. How are you?" "You look beautiful, Mrs. Jolanta." Many heads of big companies in Poland weren't as important to the general populace as I was. These big wigs had money, but I had food. So when I was speeding and a Polish policeman stopped me, the minute he recognized me, his mission changed from writing a ticket to placing an order for chickens. Eventually I became one of the richest people in my city. Even though I knew I was well off, I never thought of myself as anyone special. In my eyes, I was simply a hard worker with good morals and ethics—someone who was clean, wore pressed clothes, pleasant perfume, was well groomed, and was always on time.

After Andrew's funeral service, I went to the farm the next day because a new batch of day-old chicks had arrived. Before Andrew died, I was the workhorse of the production end and he was the brain of running the business and taking care of the massive amount of paperwork. Now I had to do everything, and I was lost. Because I would have to be handling the business end of the farm, which required that I be away from the chicken houses, I hired additional help.

Although everyone tried to convince me to close the farm, I did the opposite and made plans for expansion. I was 29 years of age and looked 18. When I went to the bank to ask about a credit line increase, the loan officer said, "You have a good record, but can your parents come here?"

I said, "Parents? I'm a married woman with a seven-year-old daughter!"

Because I kept working on the farm around the clock for three weeks without eating, my weight dropped to 100 pounds. My mother, worried about my health, took advantage of my daughter's birthday, insisting that I celebrate with them. On that day, my mother set out a sumptuous spread of food, including champagne and a mouthwatering chocolate cake adorned with candles. To appease my mother, I drank champagne and ate a piece of cake.

Two hours later, after I returned home, I began to experience sharp pains in my abdomen. When the pains worsened and I began to feel lightheaded and started perspiring, I drove myself in the early morning hours to the hospital. After a team of physicians

During this era, 1974 at age 30.

examined me and ran a series of tests, they had no idea what was ailing me. Normally they would have sent me home with medication and told me to return if my condition didn't improve. But because Andrew died in that same hospital a month earlier, the doctors felt compassionate toward me and allowed me to stay.

Their decision probably saved my life. Over the next two days, my condition showed no improvement, and despite medication, my overall health deteriorated. Having localized the problem as being in my abdominal area, the doctors elected to do an exploratory surgery. An hour later, they discovered the cause of my distress—I had a burst appendix. Thankfully, the physicians surgically intervened when they did. Had they delayed another 24 hours, I would have in all likelihood died from peritonitis, which is a general poisoning of the blood that is usually fatal. As an aside, the doctor who treated me was totally dedicated to his practice and determined that I get well, which, thanks to him, I did. Years later, the son of this doctor, who is also a physician, married my daughter Jolanta. What a small world.

When I returned to my apartment, and following some deep soul searching, I concluded that God had saved my life and that I needed to be grateful for all the blessings he had bestowed upon me. For many years, I had assumed complete control of my life. Was it possible that all those years of being a tomboy, hating rules, and being in control had resulted in my pushing God away? I began to wonder if the key aspect that had been missing in my life was God, who was needed to keep me on track and in line.

That week I returned to church and began attending morning mass, arriving an hour early at five a.m. to pray alone in the sanctuary. The following week, I was approached by a nun who asked me why I was coming every day to morning mass and praying so fervently. After she heard my story about Andrew's death and how I had almost died weeks later, she asked if I would be comfortable with her and several of her sisters coming to my home to pray.

In the week that followed, a group of nuns arrived at my

apartment every evening and soon began trying to convince me to become a nun. While initially I thought their suggestion sounded like a wonderful idea and maybe even the answer to my stressed out life (and even perhaps part of God's plan for me), I voiced my concerns about what would become of my daughter.

According to the nuns, this wouldn't be a problem. In fact, my becoming a nun would be a blessing for Jolanta, who then would be able to attend a Catholic boarding school that catered to the richest families in Europe. Jolanta would have the best of everything, including her own governess. This was starting to sound more and more like God's will for me—my daughter would be a clone of one of Maria's children in *The Sound of Music!*

I had no doubt that my mother was aware of the nuns coming every night to my apartment, which was directly across the street from my mother's home. When two days later her curiosity got the best of her, she arrived at my apartment at night unannounced and asked what was going on. I told her not to worry, that everything was fine, and that I'd explain everything later.

The following evening she arrived again, only this time she wasn't going to be put off. When I told her that I was planning on becoming a nun, it took all of her self-control and good manners to say goodnight to the nuns. When the door to my apartment closed, my mother exploded. "Are you crazy? Have you lost your mind? You almost died two weeks ago, your life gets saved, and what are you doing now? You want to become a nun? I'll give you a nun! Where's my belt? You're going to Sweden!"

So ended this chapter of God's will, if indeed my becoming a nun *was* God's will. Maybe my mother's tirade was God's will, and I'd misread everything. In any case, my mother packed my belongings and three days later drove me to Gdynia where at nine in the morning I boarded a ferry for the seven hour trip to Karlskrona, Sweden.

CHAPTER FIVE

THE SHIP CAPTAIN

The Tor Shipping Line had been established in 1966 by two Swedish companies to operate car-passenger services between Sweden, England, and the Netherlands. Shortly before my trip, Tor Line purchased two state-of-the-art ferries for the service. The new ships were the fastest and largest ferries in the world, except for the Soviet Union's *Belorussia* class vessels.

As the massive ship cruised easily on the Baltic Sea, I found my way to the dining room to have a lunch. After the maître d' sat me at a quaint table, the ship's captain walked up to me and asked if I would join him for lunch at his Captain's table. He seemed personable and overly confident, dark hair, and was slightly taller than I was. If he was handsome, I didn't notice because I was confused and somewhat startled because I didn't know this man. When I got in touch with my emotions, I realized that I felt like a prostitute and couldn't figure out why he had chosen me because I had to look terrible. I didn't care if he thought I was a prostitute. I was a lady and I wasn't about to have lunch with a total stranger. I didn't care if he was the ship's captain or owned the entire Baltic Sea.

After succinctly declining his offer, I excused myself and went to the restroom. Seeing the reflection in the mirror of my pale, gaunt look and skinny body, I broke down and cried. What did he want with me, what with all the beautiful, seemingly unattached, women walking around the ship? After fixing my makeup, I made my way to an isolated area of the ship's well-appointed lounge where I read several magazines to pass the time.

Around five o'clock that evening, I returned to the dining

room for a light supper and was seated with a group of ladies who, like myself, were traveling alone. One of the women made a reference to a bottle of cognac that had been brought to the table. Moments later, the ship's captain appeared, politely introduced himself, and then commented, "We're heading into a storm, ladies. There's no cause for alarm, but the ship is going to get rocky. Because you've all eaten dinner, you'll want to have some cognac with my compliments. It will help ward off sea sickness."

In 1974 I was 30 years of age and rarely drank. For whatever reason that escaped me at the time, I joined the women in drinking that cognac, actually taking only a few sips. To my surprise and dismay, when the captain returned a half hour later, I was tipsy and slightly thick tongued. When the captain nonchalantly invited us on a tour of the ship, the ladies accepted and I happily joined them. The ship's tour took a half hour, and all I kept saying—perhaps all I was able to say—was "Nice, nice, that's nice."

Captain Andrew's ferry.

The tour ended at the ship's bar where the captain asked me what I'd like to drink.

"Cranberry juice," I replied, thankful that I hadn't slurred those two words.

"Straight?"

Not being a drinker, I wasn't sure what he meant by that, but agreeably replied, "Yes, straight."

He shrugged with a smile, and then over the next 15 minutes engaged our group in pleasant conversation. One of the ship's crew, an officer who obviously was friends with the captain, slipped up alongside him and said, "Andrew, we're coming into Karlskrona." The man's words caused me to straighten up in my chair and direct my attention to the ship's captain, who until now had been addressed by everyone simply as "Captain."

"Excuse me, who is Andrew?" I inquired.

"I am," the captain said simply.

"Oh, *you're* Andrew?"

"Yes. Andrew is my first name. Why do you ask?"

I didn't want to tell him that my former husband was named Andrew and that he had told me for years that if anything ever happened to him that he would watch over me and wanted me to remarry as soon as possible. I wondered if my serendipitous meeting with this captain was part of my former husband "watching over me."

At eight o'clock that evening as the ship entered the harbor, the captain asked me to meet him at the top of the gangway when the passengers began leaving the ship. I told him I would, and then quickly scurried down the gangway the minute I saw my male friend waiting on the dock. One reason I ran from the captain was because the man who had come to meet the ship wanted to marry me, and I really needed to keep my life simple. While I wasn't interested in a serious relationship, I did from time to time enjoy the company of men who were intelligent and polite.

As we drove away, I saw Captain Andrew standing at the stairs, visually scanning the area. When a week later, it came time for my return trip to Poland, I purposely chose a travel day when I knew from the schedule that this particular captain wouldn't be working because I was certain he'd be checking his passenger list for me.

A few weeks after my return to Bialystok, the ship's captain found me, having obtained my address from my ticketing records. It was around Easter time when he knocked on my door and asked what I was doing for Easter. After I recovered from the initial shock of seeing him on my front porch, I told him I wasn't celebrating Easter because my husband just died, I didn't have food in the refrigerator except to feed my daughter, I had no interest in dressing up for the occasion, and most of all my mother wouldn't approve.

Since Andrew's death, I had pretty much walled off my emotions. When I heard a song that reminded me of Andrew, I turned off the radio. When the sun was shining, I closed the drapes. In my heart and soul, my life was over.

The captain wasn't going to return to his ship without a fight and suggested that we go talk with my mother. Maybe she would approve. If talking with my mother is what it would take to get rid of this persistent captain, then I was for it because I was certain that he wouldn't convince my mother. Much to my surprise, my mother thought my spending Easter with this ship captain was a wonderful idea and even packed my luggage. No doubt she was willing to try anything that might snap me out of my severe depression.

It worked. I spent Easter with the captain on his ship and was made to feel special. Besides an exquisite Easter dinner, throughout the rest of my three-day stay on the ship, the chef came to my room an hour before every meal and asked what I wanted. It felt nice that so many people cared for me and were even serving me.

Over the next several months, Andrew regularly visited my home and when he was out at sea sent me beautifully written letters that read like poetry. When he visited every two weeks,

Wedding to Captain Andrew Soysal.

he stayed in a hotel. My mother said, "What kind of life are you going to have as a single woman? You want more children. And besides, his family likes you. You're not getting younger and prettier—your imagination is growing, but your reality isn't."

I was drawn to this man because he was polite, educated, and seemed to know everything. The fact that he came from a well-established European family was icing on the cake, to quote an old cliché. When I first met him, I felt like a little girl from the village and was captivated by his many stories that he told about his worldly travels. It wasn't that I felt financially secure with him because the money I was earning from the farm provided me with an adequate income.

Most of all, what captured my heart was that he fell in love with my daughter and the two became crazy about each other. Captain Andrew never had children, which is why he was doting on Jolanta and constantly bringing her gifts from all his ship's ports of call.

Eventually the day arrived when he proposed and we were married six months after that first day he approached me on his ship and invited me to join him for lunch at his Captain's table. Andrew had many qualities that I had for a husband and father, speaking of which my daughter Jolanta was complaining more than ever that she didn't have a sibling, which was true. All of her school friends had two or three siblings, and Jolanta was by herself.

My marriage to Captain Andrew Soysal amounted to a big wedding with both families in attendance. The reception was held at an elegant private lawyer's club in Warsaw whose members all belonged to the upper class.

Within a few months, I was pregnant. Because I had previously lost a baby shortly after giving birth and Jolanta had been born premature, I was cared for by the most famous gynecologist in Poland. I ate only the healthiest of foods, and when at the farm ate outside in the forest basked by the nourishing sun. Not

My father (seated) at my daughter Jolanta's first communion. From top left: my sister Halina, friend of Andrew's, my friend Halina who later moved to the United States, and Captain Andrew. My daughter Jolanta is standing in front. At the time this photo was taken, I was in Warsaw delivering Anna.

Andrew's uncle and my favorite person in his family—Professor Albert Leskiewicz, who was a highly intelligent scientist who published 120 scientific papers and registered 15 patents.

wanting another tragedy, I went to great lengths to take excellent care of myself.

The plan was for me to deliver the baby in Warsaw where their hospital was a far better equipped than the hospital in Bialystok. Because the 125 mile trip to Warsaw would take two hours by car, I planned to drive to Warsaw a few days before my expected delivery date, particularly because Andrew was at sea and it would be necessary for my mother to stay in Bialystok to care for Jolanta.

All this changed, however, when early one evening, a full week before my delivery date, I began to feel what felt like early labor pains. This couldn't have happened at a worse time because the following day Jolanta was going to have her first communion at the Catholic Church where most of my family and Andrew's family would be in attendance. After several hours of intermittent

Jolanta's first communion.

pain, I laid down and tried to convince myself to relax and remain calm. Then at midnight, I could wait no longer. I had gone into labor and needed to get to Warsaw. I had a full tank of gas in my car, and headed off, driving above the speed limit on sheer determination and a prayer. At all costs, I wasn't going to lose another baby!

When I arrived at the hospital just under two hours later, the front of my maternity dress dressed soaked because my water had broken. The doctors were astonished that I had driven all the way from Bialystok by myself while in labor. A short while later, I gave birth to my second daughter—Anna Magdalena. After delivering Anna, and to the utter amazement of my doctor and nursing staff, I got off the delivery table and walked back to my room. After three days, my sister Alicja came with Jolanta by train to Warsaw to pick me up. On the trip home, all I could think of was how beautiful and healthy Anna was. I truly felt blessed.

No doubt when Andrew first saw the farm, he felt that I

With my sister Alicja (far right) and her first husband Bogdon. Anna is seated in the carriage that his held by my daughter Jolanta. Alicja's son Matthew, who is now a famous photographer in London, is kneeling.

ABOVE: Anna in her dog cart. BELOW: Anna six years of age.

Anna at age 7,
joins Solidarity,
holding flower.

Andrew with
Anna at age 10.

would handle the entire operation. I would have my own world on the farm, and he would have his world on the high seas. Like my mother, I was a hard worker and enjoyed my work, and I think that Andrew felt I would be satisfied with that. Besides, I would also have my family and my involvement with my church.

Andrew and I rarely saw each other because he spent most of his time at sea, and when he was home, I spent most of my time on the chicken farm. When we did see each other—often for two weeks every couple of months—he seemed more like a guest in my home. I love guests in my home, but not this. After a while, I felt more like one of his ship's crew. Worst of all, like my father, nothing was ever good enough for Andrew. He didn't like anything that was average. And I didn't have time to cater to his every need and whim, even though I understood that he was used to this, being a ship captain with a large crew of subordinates. If I was going to be with a man, then I needed to feel that I have value and purpose, and that he needs me for something. Unfortunately, after ten years of marriage, it was clear to me that Andrew didn't need me for anything. When I explained this to him, he didn't listen.

My lackluster marriage aside, I had a chicken farm to run and two daughters to raise, in addition to my sister Alicja's five-year-old son Matthew, whom I agreed to raise while my sister attended college in London.

Of course, there was always a continuing problem with the communists. Once, over a five week period, I sold enough chickens to a group of local villagers to buy a beautiful new Fiat, which was an Italian made sports car. Every year the communists audited my books, and I knew when they saw me driving around in that flashy car, they'd become suspicious about where I got the money. The reality was the communists had no way of knowing how much money I was making because none of them had the time to come to the farm and count chickens; nor did they have a clue as to how many real employees I had working for me as opposed to how many were on the books. Regardless, whenever the communists did question me about what appeared to be financial excesses, I gave them a stock answer, which was simply that I was married to a ship captain who earned a good living. Over time, I became increasingly annoyed with their meddling. As far as I was concerned, much of what they questioned me about was none of their business, and there were times when I had no compunction about telling them just that.

When I first went into the chicken business, I was told by a smart businessman to take out a personal bank loan and keep making small payments, and when that loan was paid off, take out another loan. This way the communists wouldn't suspect that I had a lot of money. Apparently I became too lax in my spending because one day I received a letter from the communists stating that I owed an outrageous amount of money in taxes.

I'd been through this fiasco before when two years earlier I applied for an apartment, and I knew how to play the game. I sent a letter stating, "Of course I'm going to pay, except first tell me why all these other people who have government owned businesses aren't paying this high tax? Why do I have to be the first?" and ended by stating, "If you don't answer my letter in 30 days, I am going to refuse to pay this tax and send a copy of this letter to the Minister of Agriculture, as well as two communist high authorities." Not surprisingly, the entire matter was quickly dismissed.

After six months, my chicken farm was running smoothly and I was able to travel. One day I was returning from Lublin, where I'd been on a short vacation, and driving to Bialystok to pick up my daughter Jolanta. We were going to attend the Sopot International Song Festival, which is an annual international song contest held in Sopot, Poland. It was the biggest song concert in Europe, and everybody who was anyone attended. I had a fancy English car—a Maurice—that broke down on my way to Bialystok and was towed to a repair shop.

After the mechanic checked into the problem, he told me

that the car couldn't be fixed for several days because he needed to order a special part. I called home and arranged for a friend to pick up Jolanta and take her to his house, and that I'd be home late and would call him in the morning.

While I was standing beside the road outside the repair shop trying to figure out the best way to get to Bialystok, a long, gleaming white Peugeot pulled to a stop beside me. Moments later, the front passenger window slid down, and I found myself looking at a strikingly handsome Italian man who asked if I needed a lift.

My initial reaction was that I didn't want to accept his offer because I didn't speak any foreign languages except Hungarian and Russian. Before I could respond, however, he got out of the car, opened the passenger door, and in a gentlemanly manner helped me in, while now speaking to me in Polish.

A short ways down the road he introduced himself as Giovanni and asked where I was going. I told him that I was going to Bialystok. As it turned out, he was driving to Warsaw. We got along so famously that he drove me all the way home. During the drive, I learned that he was H.E. Chev. Giovanni Ferrara, Grand Prior of Italy, a highly influential person who worked for Chevalier Roland Valerio Boesso KLJ (Grand Priority of Italy) who was a decorated WWII Marine and resistance fighter, ran television stations and was involved in politics, and was the founder of the regional newspaper *Alto Adige*.

Because the hour was late when Giovanni and I arrived in Bialystok, and I knew he was weary from the long drive, I told him he was welcome to stay overnight in my apartment.

Tired from the long day and evening, I showered and then went to my room. Ten minutes later, I heard Giovanni showering, after which he walked into my room with only a towel wrapped around his waist, seemingly ready to retire for the night. I could hardly believe his audacity.

"Excuse me," I said sternly. "You see those doors? Get out of this room!"

With a shocked expression on his face and without so much

Above: Rolando and girlfriend (later wife). Below: Giovani in Balsano North Italy reporting on event.

as a peep, he sheepishly backed into the hallway and walked to the guest bedroom.

The following morning, Giovanni awoke early, made his bed, and was sitting patiently in the armchair when I knocked on the door and entered the guest bedroom. Springing to his feet, he began apologizing profusely. I told him everything was all right and that I understood his behavior the night before was the result of generations of Italian blood coursing in his veins. We laughed, and he said he wanted to take me to breakfast. When I agreed, he said, "But you know, I've only known you for a day, and it would look better if you drove my car and I was a passenger because if it's an Italian car and an Italian driver in Poland—"

"What?" I said, interrupting him. "You're in my city and they're not going to think anything. But okay, as you wish."

I was surprised that he was concerned about what the communists might think, but didn't pursue it. A short while later, we arrived at my farm where I gave him a grand tour. He was impressed, to say the least. I suppose in Italy, most women are homemakers. Those who did enter into the workforce, work for someone else. It was rare that he met a woman who was the head person of a business enterprise as big as my farm.

"Do you have an accountant and a lawyer?" he asked. My sense was he was trying to figure out if the brains of the operation was actually a silent, absentee partner.

"No. I do everything. I'm the lawyer and the accountant." The truth was that after Andrew died, I had an attorney, but I fired him because he was a meek person whose stock defense was to paint me as a helpless, grieving widow, and from that point on I represented myself—and never lost a case.

Giovanni and I spent the rest of the day driving around Bialystok, then returned to my apartment where he cooked a wonderful Italian dinner for me. Later in the evening he said as he took my hand, "Jolanta, you're a very special person. I want to invite you to Italy. Have you been?"

That was quite an offer. Up to this point, I had done considerable travel throughout Europe, but had yet to visit Italy. I had no idea how serious he was about his invitation, but gave him my information. He planned to spend the night and then drive me back to the auto shop to get my car. An hour before retiring, the man who was taking care of my daughter arrived with Jolanta and immediately pulled me into my bedroom and closed the door. "Whose car is that outside?" he demanded. I had no idea that he became jealous upon seeing Giovanni in the living room.

"It belongs to my friend. Giovanni, the gentleman outside in—"

"Tell him to go."

"He wants to drive me back to Gdansk to get my car."

"No, he can go. I will take you. This does not look good this strange man staying in your apartment while Jolanta is here."

I suppose there was some sense to what he was saying. I returned to the living room and told Giovanni that I had transportation to the auto shop the following morning. He said that he would see me in Italy. I walked him to his car, and we said our farewells. I never expected to see or hear from him again.

When I returned to my apartment, I found sitting on a table in the entryway a black velvet jewelry box that contained a stunning diamond and emerald necklace—along with a nice note from Giovani thanking me for my hospitality. Suddenly I was hit with the notion that perhaps I hadn't seen or heard the last from my newfound Italian friend.

When my husband Andrew came for vacation, I told him about Giovanni and his invitation to Italy. Andrew said, "You're so naïve. I'll bet he invites a dozen ladies a week to Italy and not one ever hears from him again. Did you tell him you're married?"

"I didn't have to. I'm sure he figured it out. Anyway, we're just friends."

A short while later, a letter arrived from Giovanni, who reiterated his invitation for me to come to Italy. I showed the letter to my husband. "So, no one ever hears from him again?"

Andrew perused the letter several times, and then announced, "You're not going!"

"Oh, yes, I'm going, my dear."

"No, you're not!" he repeated.

"And why am I not going? Tell me. I don't know what you do on your ship, but whatever it is, it's okay with me because I have a ship captain for a husband." I kept looking at him, waiting for his response, but he knew better and kept silent.

My husband wasn't the worst hurdle. I needed to convince the communists to issue me a travel visa to Italy. I suppose it should have come as no surprise that, upon receiving my visa application, the communists summoned me several times to its passport office. During my first two visits, the official's line of questioning was vague. On my third visit, I finally voiced my objection. "You keep inviting me here, three times now. Apparently you have a problem with my traveling to Italy, so fine—I'm not going to Italy!"

"No, no," the official replied. "You're going to go to Italy."

Although the communists ruled Poland with a strong hand, they were careful to not upset its citizens if it could be avoided. And they knew that I was a successful businesswoman with many connections.

"Fine. So when will that be? Why do you keep asking me to come to your office and then talk to me so strangely?"

The official considered me for a long while, then said, "Well, there is some concern about you being married to a ship captain."

Surely they knew my husband was a communist. He had to be if he wanted to have the job of a ship captain. What they didn't know was that my husband didn't like the communists or communism.

"And why is that a problem?"

"Well, you could give him… information. The fact that he travels a lot outside of Poland would make—"

"What information? I run a chicken farm? You think I'm a spy? When my husband comes for vacation, we talk about food and our three children."

The official paused for a long while, and then slowly said, "Do you know an Italian by the name of Giovanni?"

So that was it. The communists had been told about my driving around Bialystok with this politically influential Italian.

"Yes, I know him. I met him recently. He's a lawyer."

"He's a lawyer and a... journalist," he said pointedly.

"Good, he's a lawyer and a journalist, so what's wrong?"

We continued to play out the game for another 20 minutes, after which the man was convinced, at least to his satisfaction, that I wasn't an international spy who was passing secrets to the United States.

This wasn't the first time the communists hauled me into their office. Because I wanted my daughters to look nice, I often took them shopping in Warsaw where we stayed at the Hotel Bristol, which was the best hotel. A week after we returned from one of our shopping sprees, I was summoned to the Polish Police Department where an official asked what I was doing in Warsaw.

"I was at a hotel," I said.

"Yes, I know. An expensive hotel."

"Yes, I work hard to afford to stay there."

"Do you know how many famous people stay there from all over the world?"

"I don't care who stays there. I went there with my daughters to shop."

Again, their grilling went nowhere. There were a half dozen of this type of snoop by the communists. They were determined to control everyone's life, which ultimately made the majority of Polish citizens paranoid—and angry.

Upon finally being issued a passport by the Polish government, I traveled to Italy where I was reunited with Giovanni. Some of my friends and family felt that I might have second thoughts because I was a married woman. But this didn't happen. Giovanni and I were friends and I saw nothing wrong with traveling to see him and fulfilling a long time dream to go to Italy.

Following the short plane flight to Milano, I finally landed and was reunited with Giovanni, who turned out to have a jealous streak. During the flight, I had struck up friendly conversation with a handsome airline captain from Rome. At first, I tried to ignore him, but he was persistent. When Giovanni arrived at the airport, he found me sitting with this airline captain who had invited me to lunch in Rome. He also offered me his apartment when he wasn't there, as well as his chauffeur. When I introduced this captain to Giovani, I could read Giovani's reaction, which seemed to convey that I didn't need him because I had found someone else. Sensing Giovani's discomfort, this captain invited us to La Scala for dinner and an evening at the opera. Determined to not be outdone by this fellow Italian, Giovani politely turned down the offer and then during my stay took me to the opera, which was nothing less than enchanting.

After collecting my luggage and leaving the airport, to my surprise, Giovani drove me to a sprawling villa that was perched atop a mountain and had a breathtaking panoramic view of the mountains. The three-bedroom villa was located in the quaint town of Bolzano, was exquisitely furnished, and had a resident maid who would take care of me during my stay.

In Sicily, Italy with five friends and Roland's girlfriend.

"I guess you'll be living here all by yourself," he said. He had earlier mentioned his surprise that I hadn't brought my daughter and mother with me.

"I suppose I'll just have to suffer," I said laughing.

After Giovani left, I sat on a magnificent sofa that was part of a four-piece set made by Italian craftsman Luigi Frullini, whose works were inspired by the carved pieces of the Italian Renaissance. I sat there for the longest time, totally breathless, trying to figure out why Giovanni had gone to all this trouble. Perhaps I knew the reason and was slow to accept it. I had for some time become known for my naivety. Anyway, whatever the reason, I was looking forward to a wonderful month in that palatial villa!

The next morning, Giovanni arrived with flowers and groceries. After preparing a delectable breakfast that we ate on the veranda that featured beautiful Italian tile, gardens, and a fountain. Then afterwards, we drove to Milan, which is the main industrial, commercial, and financial center of Italy. Its business district hosts the Borsa Italiana (Italy's main stock exchange) and the headquarters of the largest national banks and companies. The city is a major world fashion and design capital. Milan's museums, theaters, and landmarks (including the Milan Cathedral, the fifth-largest cathedral in the world, and Santa Maria delle Grazie, decorated with Leonardo da Vinci paintings, and a UNESCO World Heritage Site) attract over eight million visitors annually.

Throughout the drive and tour, I had so many questions— what is this? What is that? I was completely captivated by a brain that was asking like a huge sponge. Two hours later, we drove up into the mountains to an antique hotel that was where Winston Churchill had stayed near the end of WWII. The entire hotel was surrounded by an enormous wall of flowers.

"Are you ready for lunch?" Giovanni asked.

"Sure," I replied. "I'm starving."

We entered the hotel and he took me to a huge, stately restaurant that was empty except for a long table that was beautifully set for 40 guests. Lit candles and bottles of wine adorned the table of

Italian linen, sparkling crystal, and polished silver.

"What is this? Is there going to be a wedding here?"

"No, no," he replied. "Come with me."

We walked into an anteroom that featured an enormous cathedral ceiling. The eyes of 40 gathered guests suddenly turned to greet me. Among the highly esteemed guests was one of the most important and powerful men in Italy, Giovanni's boss—Rolando Valerio Boesso. When Rolando introduced himself and his girlfriend Brigitte, I didn't hear a word because I was in shock from so many people having come here on my behalf. What followed was a luncheon that I shall never forget. Everyone was elegantly dressed, the food and service were superb, as well as the tuxedoed string quartet playing Italian music. At the end of the lunch, one of the female guests asked me what my plans were in Italy. Before I could answer, Giovanni stood and said, "Tomorrow we're going to Rome!"

The following day when we arrived in Rome, Giovanni took me to St. Peter Basilica where I was met by a Polish nun and priest who took me on a tour of St. Peter Basilica and described everything to me in Polish. St. Peter's Basilica is the most re-

Saint Peter's Basilica.

nowned work of Renaissance architecture and is one of the two largest churches in the world and is regarded as one of the holiest Catholic shrines. The Basilica is the burial site of its namesake St. Peter, one of the Apostles of Jesus Christ, as well as the first Pope and Bishop of Rome. According to tradition, many Popes have been interred at St. Peter's since the Early Christian period.

I felt as if God were watching over me. I told the priest and nun about my first husband Andrew's death; and that the second anniversary of that tragedy was in two days. I prayed at the Polish altar for my daughters to be in those places and asked the priest if it were possible to have a mass in St. Peter Cathedral for Andrew. Earlier, unbeknownst to me, he had discussed the possibility with his superiors and obtained permission. This mass was for Andrew's soul—wherever he is—and it is an important tradition for Catholics. Because of this I was suddenly struck with the notion that this was my mission as part of my travel to Italy.

I enjoyed standing out in Italy. Practically everywhere I went in Italy people would turn and look at me. This was because I was blonde with blue eyes, which was rare in Italy where practically everyone—except for a small segment of Northern Italians—had dark hair and dark eyes. I didn't see anything exceptional about my coloring, but to Giovanni I was special. While I was in Italy, I did a photographic shoot that appeared in *Bizarre* magazine that Giovanni arranged through his nephew who was a professional photographer. After the shoot, Giovani's nephew suggested that I stay in Italy and pursue a career as a model.

"What? A shrimp like me?" I said.

"No, no," the nephew replied, "a model for eyes, lips, and hands."

After I left Italy, and in the months that followed, I realized that the Polish government had been right about Giovanni's interest in me, because on the 3rd of May he arrived in Poland with a professional cameraman. A week later on the 10th of May was an anti-communist demonstration, and Giovanni knew this and asked me if they could film me talking about what the Polish people thought about communism. Months earlier, throughout my stay in Italy, he had arranged for me to take a crash course in Italian so that we could communicate better, and now I suspected that these lessons were meant for this interview that had been planned all along.

I also learned that when I first met Giovanni when my car broke down on my way to Bialystok, he was coming back from the apartment of his fiancée.

The necklace of emeralds and diamonds that he gave me was supposed to be a wedding gift for her, but because she was a devout Catholic and insisted on many conditions, he decided at the last minute that she wasn't for him. And so when we met, he was driving home with a broken heart. Besides the bracelet, all the money that Giovanni spent on me, including my travel expenses and the rental of the villa, was paid for by Rolando, in addition to all the meals, the opera, and nightclubs. The last time I heard from Giovanni, he wrote telling me that he could not see me again because he had a wife, as well as a girlfriend.

In the weeks that followed Giovanni's departure from Poland, I concluded that I had been in the right place at the right time. I loved his company because I loved to dance. I could dance for hours by myself in the park with music; and Giovanni and his friends gave me champagne and fine food and they were all such elegant company.

With Giovanni now a fleeting memory, I again focused on my family and my work. Then in October 1978, what is arguably the greatest moment in the history of Poland's Catholic Church occurred. Months earlier Pope Paul VI died at the age of 80, sending millions of Catholics throughout the world into a state of mourning. Then in September the newly elected Pope John Paul I died unexpectedly at the age of 65 after only 34 days in office, again leaving the Church without a pope. Then on October 16,

1978 Karol Cardinal Wojtyla of Poland was elected as the new Pope as John Paul II. On the day Catholics got their first Polish Pope, I stopped breathing along with the rest of Poland. What a foundation I felt I now had. I remember this glorious event as if it were yesterday. I felt like heaven was open for all of Poland. As the Supreme Pontiff of the Roman Catholic Church, Pope John Paul II soon addressed Central and Eastern Europe, saying with regard to communism, "Do not be afraid. Let your spirit descend and change the image of this land."

Pope John Paul II.

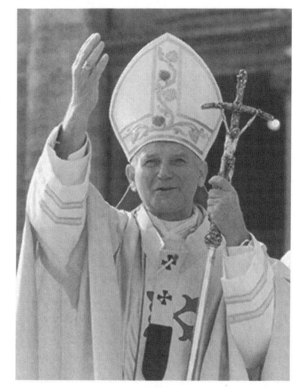

CHAPTER SIX

AMERICA

I n late 1981, conditions in Poland reached the boiling point. A year earlier, disgruntled labor workers formed their own independent pro-democratic trade union "Solidarity" that became a major political force. Faced with the threat of a Soviet ordered Warsaw pact invasion of Poland if this pro-democracy movement could not be crushed, on December 13, 1981 Poland's president Wojcech Jaruzelski had little choice but to order that Poland be placed under martial law.

Immediately, "Solidarity" was banned and its leaders jailed. Thousands of soldiers in military vehicles appeared on the streets of every major city. A curfew was imposed, the national borders sealed, airports closed, and road access to main cities was restricted. Telephone lines were disconnected, mail subjected to postal censorship, and classes in schools and universities suspended.

In addition, the government imposed a six-day work week while the mass media, public services, healthcare services, power stations, coal mines, seaports, train stations, and key factories were placed under military management. As part of the crackdown, media and educational institutions underwent "verification," a process that tested each employee's attitude towards the regime and to the Solidarity movement. As a result, thousands of journalists, teachers, and professors were banned from their professions. Military courts were established to bypass the normal court system, to imprison those spreading so-called "false information."

Restrictions led to severe economic consequences. Major price increases resulted in a drop in wages. The resulting economic crisis led to the rationing of most products and materials, in-

Polish American Congress (PAC) "Solidarity Express" humanitarian food shipments to Poland in 1981.

cluding basic foodstuffs. Coupons were needed to buy cigarettes and clothes; stamps were needed to purchase alcohol and gasoline.

As a consequence of economic hardship and political repression, an exodus of Poles saw 700,000 of its citizens emigrating to the West between 1981 and 1989. A number of international flights were high jacked by those fleeing the country. The majority who left were young and well educated people who did not foresee political or economic change. The mainstream left to Germany, Austria, or through the temporary camps in Italy to Canada, Australia, or the United States.

Sorrowfully, although I had witnessed years of Poland eroding under the harsh dictates of the communists, along with most of Poland's citizens, our president imposing martial law took me totally by surprise. Essentially, my world collapsed. Prior to martial law, the communists tricked me into working hard with a promise of early retirement. When martial law was enacted, the communists closed my chicken farm because Poland didn't produce chicken food, but instead exported it from other countries. As a result, I found myself unemployed and having to support three children—Jolanta and Anna, and my nephew Matthew.

ABOVE TOP: Poland President Wojcech Jaruzelski. ABOVE: World headlines Poland under martial law.

Martial law enforcement.

Polish citizens waiting in line for food.

Over the next several years, I became increasingly concerned that the Soviet Union fully intended to take over Poland. Worried sick over the future of my children, I became convinced that I needed to get them out of Poland. In addition, I wanted to get my parents to a safe haven, but they were getting up in years and became anxious at the thought of leaving their home and business, which was a small deli. Although I had friends in Germany, Italy, France, and London, I chose to emigrate to the United States because so many Poles were going to America.

I knew little about the United States. My only connection was a friend named Halina, who lives in New York. She operated a successful salon in Poland and ten years earlier traveled to New York where she worked as a hairdresser on First Avenue and 14th Street. Because I had helped care for her parents after she left Poland for the United States, to return the favor, Halina now invited me to stay in her apartment in New York. Beautiful, well educated, extremely personable and charming, I knew Halina would be the perfect connection. Even to this day she is one of the top cosmetologists in Manhattan.

In order to expedite my leaving Poland, I felt it would help to divorce my husband. Among other things, being single would make it easier for me to obtain a green card in the United States, which was essential to being hired to work. Although many people told me that the easiest way to obtain a green card in the United States was to marry an American citizen, this option was by no means a top priority.

When I told Andrew about the divorce, he said, "Oh, my God, what am I going to do?"

"Nothing," I said calmly. "It's a fake divorce. After we've been divorced for two weeks, we can change it back." I later learned this was untrue and that our divorce would legally be final.

Andrew wouldn't hear of it and started yelling. It was terrible. My mother was upset, as well as my sister in London, and just about everyone else. But I had made up my mind, and it was done. Captain Andrew turned out to not be right for me or—

Goodbye party prior to leaving for America with radio/TV personality in Bialystok.

better said—we weren't right for each other. I needed a man who would stay with me and share my problems and joys in life.

As the day approached when I would leave for the United States, I cried all night. Although my mother agreed to watch over my children, who would also be provided with a maid and housekeeper, my separation from them would turn out to be one of the most difficult and emotionally painful life experiences.

My plane flight to the United States went much faster than I had expected. As the plane began making its gradual descent on its approach JFK airport, the pilot announced over the intercom, "Welcome to the United States of America." While many of the US citizens traveling on this flight continued to read their newspapers and such, many who were traveling to America for the first time were deeply moved by the pilot's words. Tears fell from the eyes of many passengers who rushed to the aircraft's windows to gaze down upon the signature landmarks of New York—the Statue of Liberty, the Brooklyn Bridge, and the Empire State Building. Because I was too preoccupied on my mission to save my children from an impending invasion by the Soviet Union, I never raced to those windows. My only reaction was that I hoped for a safe and quick landing so that I could begin the job that I came to do.

After clearing customs and while waiting for Halina to arrive, I spotted my favorite French perfume in one of the airport stores and couldn't resist buying it for $40—which left me with a grand total of $60! Back then, Polish citizens were allowed to bring no more than the Polish equivalent of $100 into the United States.

After 20 minutes passed without sign of Halina, I worried that she had forgotten about me. I didn't know how to make a phone call in the United States because I didn't know how pay phones worked, didn't know the currency, and spoke only a few words of English. I stood in the middle of the baggage area for another ten minutes, growing panicky, when a man walked up to me and asked me in Polish, "Are you Jolanta?"

"Yes!" I blurted out loudly as I threw my arms around him. "Thank God, you saved me!" It was true. Had there been no one to pick me up, I would have been immediately deported back to Poland and my tourist visa revoked indefinitely.

My first impression of America was heartwarming. Although I'd never been to the United States, when I walked out to the bustling street at the airport, I thought to myself *thank God I'm home.* I loved New York from my first breath and knew that it was destined to become my favorite city in the entire world, which turned out to be true. My inner familiarity with the city was so profound that I wondered if I'd in some way been there before because everything and everyone felt so familiar. As we drove away from the airport, it suddenly dawned on me why I loved this city so much—it was because New York was bigger than me!

Halina's small apartment was in Manhattan on 2nd Avenue and 27th Street. Manhattan is often said to be the economic and

With my friend Halina.

cultural center of the United States and serves as home to the United Nations Headquarters, as well as the world's two largest stock exchanges, the New York Stock Exchange and NASDAQ.

"I'm inviting you for three months," Halina said. "Everything is on me. So you can just relax."

Halina was under the impression that I had come to New York to vacation because I had only a 90-day tourist visa that didn't permit me to work without papers.

Having a green card would allow me to freely travel back and forth from Poland. With a visa, once you leave, the visa expires. I wouldn't get another visa for a long time from Poland. With a green card, I could come and go both ways. Because obtaining a green card was so important, prior to my arrival in America, Halina had arranged for a Polish attorney to help me through the process.

My plan was simple. Until I obtained a green card, I would find nominal work from an employer who would pay me under the table. This would hopefully result in my being able to afford a small apartment, and once a green card was issued I would procure a higher paying job that would eventually allow me to begin processing my children to come to the United States. Although my basic plan sounded good on paper, I had absolutely no idea how I was going to accomplish any of its lofty goals. The stark reality was that I was a chicken farmer from Poland who landed in New York with no money, no profession, and didn't speak English. After I settled in at Halina's apartment, we sat in her small living room enjoying a glass of wine.

"So what do you intend to do?" Halina asked.

"Anything," I replied eagerly.

"Anything means nothing. I mean realistically."

After another sip of wine and a moment of thought, I replied, "I could drive a car for someone."

Halina smiled, her expression suggesting that she knew something I didn't.

"This is New York," she replied forebodingly. "It's not Poland."

"I have an international driver's license."

"You'll need more than that. Anyway, you don't speak English."

Before I came to the United States, my sister Alicja told me not to worry, that my not knowing English wouldn't be a problem, that there was a large Polish community living in Greenpoint, New York and that many had lived there for 50 years and didn't speak a word of English. Greenpoint is the northernmost neighborhood in the New York City borough of Brooklyn, New York. Known for its large Polish immigrant and Polish-American community, it is often referred to as "Little Poland." Notable individuals who were born in or lived in Greenpoint include actress Mae West, actor Mickey Rooney, bank robber Willie Sutton, and writer Henry Miller.

On my second day in New York, I went to Greenpoint. Later, when a friend asked me what I thought of this Polish community, I said, "Thank God when I arrived in New York yesterday that my friend Halina didn't live in Greenpoint, because had she lived there, I wouldn't have even opened my luggage because I would have returned that hour to Poland, the place was that terrible."

By the end of my first week in New York, Halina made an appointment for me to clean the apartment of an elderly, well-established Italian lady named Angela Costa who lived nearby. When I left Poland, it was the dead of winter, and I was told that winter in New York wasn't much better. Needless to say, I didn't pack a maid's uniform or even anything remotely close to one.

Upon arriving at the woman's apartment building that was located on 1st Avenue and 14th Street and being cleared through the main lobby, I took the elevator to the third floor and walked down the hallway to Mrs. Costa's apartment and rang the bell. Moments later, a thin, conservatively dressed Italian lady opened the door and stared at me. She appeared confused as she considered her maid temp who had arrived wearing an expensive woolen pant suit, knee-high black leather boots, and a fur coat.

"Jolanta?" the woman finally asked, her eyes squinting as if trying to focus on her elegantly dressed maid.

Thankfully, I spoke Italian and was able to explain my eccentric apparel. Over the next two hours, I cleaned Mrs. Costas' apartment (I was a wizard from years of cleaning my chicken houses) as if giving her a grand tour of a museum. Much to her amazement, and because of my travels throughout Europe and especially Italy, I was familiar with many of the pieces of fine art that hung on her walls, her photo album of the Vatican, and most of her expensive Italian wines.

When I finished cleaning the woman's apartment, she mentioned that she had prepared a lunch for me, apparently having forgotten what she had thrown together for "the maid." When she opened her refrigerator and realized what she had prepared, she quickly glanced at the nearby trash receptacle, and then placed the foil-covered meal back into the refrigerator and closed the refrigerator door.

"Do you have anything in particular that you'd like for lunch?"

After giving it thought, I replied with full honesty. I felt the woman deserved as much. "Shrimp cocktail and red wine."

Mrs. Costa stared at me for a moment, and then smiled. "A perfect choice," she said. "Give me a few minutes. I'll be right back." Ten minutes later, we were sitting down enjoying a glass of wine and eating shrimp that the woman obtained from a neighbor.

"So tell me,' the woman asked between shrimps, "why are you cleaning houses?"

"You don't like my work?"

"I love your work, but why are you cleaning?"

"I don't speak English," I said in Italian. "I arrived here this week and spent most of my money on perfume."

The woman looked dumbfounded. After she listened to my explanation as to why I had brought only $100 into the United States, she gave me the contact information for an English class in which I enrolled the next day, further suggesting that I never clean apartments again.

I was often tense because I worried that someone would talk to me and I'd look stupid because I didn't understand them. Weeks later, while riding the subway home, I noticed an overweight woman who looked like a homeless person. As physically unattractive as she was, she spoke perfect English. Because of this, I would have traded my comparatively beautiful appearance for her beautiful English, and at that moment vowed to redouble my efforts to learn the language.

The following day, I started memorizing 50 English words every night before going to sleep. After a month, I had learned 2,000 words. When I met people whom I hadn't seen in a while, I'd enter into conversation with them and they'd say, "You speak English!"

After realizing that I wasn't going to finance an apartment in New York by being a part-time cleaning lady, I went in search of other work. Four days later, I was introduced to an elderly Polish man who was in need of a chauffeur. Charles L. Schreiber, who was the founder and president of Royal Farms Dairy, had immigrated to the United States when he was 13 years old with nothing more than a worn suitcase stuffed with secondhand clothing. Decades later, he could stuff ten suitcases with hundred dollar bills from his chain of successful grocery stores located throughout New York with headquarters in Brooklyn.

Mr. Schreiber was 85 years old, short, overweight, and had recently been operated on for a brain tumor, which was probably why he occasionally acted strangely. Because of his failing health, he needed someone to drive him to business meetings, doctor appointments, and social functions.

Mr. Schreiber lived in Flatbush, which was an area populated after World War II by immigrant Jews and Italians. I interviewed for the job on Friday morning, and when I returned to Halina's apartment around noon, I learned that Mr. Schreiber had called and said that I had the job and needed to start work that night, not Monday morning. Within the hour, Halina drove me back to Mr. Schreiber's home, which was a two-story, four bedroom house with nice gardens and decorated like most traditional Jewish homes.

Within a short while of my arrival, Mr. Shreiber handed me the keys to his Cadillac Fleetwood Brougham d'Elegance, which was actually a short limousine and asked that I drive him to his synagogue where he dined with his many Jewish friends every Friday night. Although I had driven an assortment of standard cars and trucks in Poland, and occasionally drove luxury cars in Europe, I'd never been behind the wheel of a car this size and whose dashboard resembled that of a jet plane. Furthermore, I had never before driven a car equipped with an automatic transmission. After depositing Mr. Shreiber in back, I discovered how to adjust the front seat and rearview mirror and headed for Ocean Parkway.

Shreiber's 1987 Cadillac Fleetwood Brougham.

After living in New York for many years, I can personally attest to the fact that there is truth to the age-old New York adage that advises "If you really don't have to drive in New York, don't." Most people who are new to New York are advised to get a professional to do the driving for them—a cab, a car service, or at the very least, a friend or relative who is local. There is good reason for this. Driving in New York can be quite intimidating. There are about 750,000 vehicles descending upon the little island of Manhattan every day. These vehicles tend to move fast, often at very close quarters, cut into each other's path, and generally leave no margins for error. New Yorkers who cut in front of other drivers aren't rude. They are simply going for "premium" road space that is there for the taking. The New York driver mentality is "If you really wanted that space, there wouldn't be any there right now."

The above is a great description of my first experience driving Mr. Schreiber's limousine in the bustling streets of New York City. The experience was similar to what I witnessed later at Coney Island of children who wildly drove electric powered bumper cars that whizzed along a metallic floor. Besides the hectic beehive of New York drivers, Mr. Schreiber was the worst backseat driver in the history of backseat driving. He simply could not keep quiet. He gave (often shouted) directions and corrections throughout my first drive, often frantically flailing his skinny arms and reaching over my seat in an attempt to either grab the steering wheel or blare the horn. Needless to say, I was greatly relieved when I finally arrived at the synagogue and Mr. Schreiber had a glass of Mogen David wine.

Over the next three weeks, I thankfully became proficient driving Mr. Schreiber's sleek Cadillac in hectic New York traffic. Fortunately, before my stay at Halina's apartment ended, Mr. Schreiber offered me a nice room and bath at his house where he lived alone. Because he employed a housekeeper who came every morning and left after fixing Mr. Schreiber dinner, I wasn't required to cook and clean.

Everything ran smoothly for several weeks, and then one night around three in the morning, Mr. Schreiber came to my bedroom wearing a shiny pair of pajamas, woolen robe, and shuffling along in leather slippers like a 100-year-old George Burns. Arriving at my bedside, he sat on the edge of my bed. I stared at him for a long while. He seemed slightly confused, and I wondered if he was sleepwalking. "Mr. Schreiber, this is my bedroom."

He murmured to himself without acknowledging me, and then pulled back the covers and slipped a leg onto the mattress, clearly intending to get into my bed. Almost instinctively, I kicked him and he fell to the floor. Terrified that I'd killed him, I let out a loud shriek. Leaning forward, I said in a soft voice, "Mr. Schreiber? Mr. Schreiber?" Moments later, he opened his eyes and smiled weakly, then curled up on the floor as if going to sleep. Not knowing whether to call the paramedics or the police or Halina—or all three—and satisfied that he was all right, I went to the kitchen and made myself a cup of coffee while I collected my thoughts.

A couple minutes later, I looked up and saw Mr. Schreiber leaning against the kitchen doorway. He stared at me for a long while, seemingly trying to gain his bearings, then asked "What are you doing?"

I sat motionless for several moments, then replied, "I'm making coffee."

A faint smile suddenly turned the corners of the old man's mouth. "Oh. Make some for me, will you?"

There was a slight twinkle in his eyes, and I wondered if he had any recollection of trying to crawl into my bed ten minutes earlier and my kicking him onto the floor.

"How do you like your coffee?" I replied, not knowing what else to say.

"Cream and a little sugar."

I made his coffee and we sat together at the kitchen table. He fell into thought for a long while, then said, "You're stupid. A girl like you shouldn't be a chauffeur. You should have your own chauffeur."

I said, "Mr. Schreiber, what do you want from me?"

"I want you to be my girlfriend," he replied.

I had no doubt that at his age and his deteriorated health that he no romantic interest in me, but I decided to amuse him. "Mr. Schreiber, why didn't you tell me when you interviewed me that you wanted to hire a prostitute?"

"This is different."

"Mr. Schreiber, I want to tell you, you don't have enough money to buy me because I'm not for sale. Okay, next."

That was the end of the conversation. Then a month later he arrived in my bedroom, sat on the edge of the bed, and again tried to crawl under the covers. As before, I kicked him, and he fell to the floor. Ten minutes later we were again in the kitchen with me asking him how he liked his coffee.

Schreiber finally said, "Jolanta, you have to go."

While I agreed with Mr. Schreiber that we couldn't continue experiencing these bizarre evenings and that he might be better off with another driver, I was concerned about being unemployed on such short notice because it was difficult for someone in my situation to find work. I was grateful that Mr. Schreiber understood this and happily gave me a fair severance pay.

By the end of the week I'd found a single apartment in Brighton Beach, New York, which was a safe Russian community. My

Brighton Beach.

apartment felt like a large shoebox—one room, small kitchen and shower—but I made it look beautiful with new paint and decorations. Brighton Beach is located in the southern portion of the New York City borough of Brooklyn, along the Coney Island Peninsula. It is a summer destination for New York City residents due to its beaches along the Atlantic Ocean. What I loved about living in Brighton Beach was spending time at neighboring Coney Island.

When I moved into my apartment, I hadn't heard the last from Mr. Schreiber who told me his heart was going to be broken and to take whatever I wanted. "What are you talking about?" I asked on the day I left.

"You don't have anything. You don't have towels. You don't have glasses. Take what you need." At his continued insistence, while moving out, he meticulously divided one towel for him, one towel for me; one glass for him, one for me. Two weeks later, when I arrived home late one night, I played a message on my answering machine from Mr. Schreiber that stated it was important that I return his call. When I called early the next morning, he said, "Jolanta, can you come over and bring me the black towel, and I'll give you the red one?"

After I left Mr. Schreiber's employ, we remained good friends. Because I was concerned about his care, I found a competent Polish woman to live with him until a heart attack took his life three months later.

The longer I stayed in New York, the more I missed my family. Back then, there wasn't an Internet that provided instant free access with anyone throughout the world. All I had was my telephone and letters. To my surprise, I didn't miss anything about Poland except my mother and my children. I was grateful that in the event an emergency arose with my family, I was available to them by telephone. At that time, the cost of a transatlantic call was expensive. One night when Anna was sick, I ended up talking with her until she finally fell asleep. When the bill arrived two weeks later, that one call was $600. I desperately missed Anna, who wasn't yet in her teen years, and worked to earn money just to hear her voice and send her packages with toys and clothes in the hope of making her happy. At that time, my daughter Jolanta was away at college studying to be a dentist. Although I was extremely proud of her accomplishments and missed her terribly, I wasn't as concerned about her well-being as I was about Anna's.

When I lived in Brighton Beach, I got a job at a famous mafia-owned Russian restaurant where I worked nights and usually didn't get home until one in the morning. During the day I attended English class in Manhattan. Russian and Polish are separate languages, and I speak both. Although initially I applied for a waitress position, because I wanted to be the best waitress, I asked to begin working in the kitchen as a sous chef preparing salads.

One night when I'd worked overtime, I clocked out and was preparing to leave when one of the Russian ladies stopped me. When I asked what she wanted, she said, "Don't leave yet. I need you to help me clean the refrigerator."

I had already taken off my uniform and had my coat on.

"I've finished work. I'm going home."

The woman became irate. "You Polish people think you're all a bunch of prima donnas."

My blood boiled. "What do you want from Polish people?"

Since arriving in New York and becoming acquainted with the Russians who were living in Brighton Beach, I began to wonder if their hostility toward Polish people had to do with the years of Soviet occupation of Poland, both during and following WWII. Before she could answer, I grabbed a wet rag and slapped her face with it, then turned and stormed out.

The next day when I didn't show up for work, the owner called and asked what had happened the previous night.

"Ask Tatianna," I replied.

The owner checked into the matter, then called back and said he would fire Tatianna, give me a raise, and promote me to a waitress position if I'd return to work. But I was done and didn't go back.

Within a week I procured another job tending bar and continued with my English class in Manhattan. In addition, I enrolled in cosmetology school that required me to attend classes in the morning. In the evening, I tended bar. When the bar closed, I traveled home on the subway, often sleeping among total strangers, some of whom were truly ominous looking. Upon arriving home, I'd collapse in bed. Early the next morning, I'd shower, fix my hair and makeup, get dressed, and begin my school and work all over again. Although I was living in New York at the height of Saturday night fever, and was in walking distance of some of the most famous and popular disco clubs, I had no time for such fun and no social life. All that mattered was making something of myself so that I could one day bring my family to America. Later there would be time to celebrate.

Mine was a hectic existence, but I was determined to reach

With friends at my bartending job.

to learn the profession of cosmetology and perfect my English so that I could continue earning money to pay my bills and send money to Poland. I never lived in a basement or Greenpoint, but always had a nice, clean place. Sometimes when I was physically and emotionally exhausted, I'd remind myself that when someone is on an airplane and a problem arises and an oxygen mask falls into view, that person first places the mask on themselves before then placing in on their children And so this is the way I thought—I needed to take care of myself first before I could help my children.

In order to save money, I gave up my apartment at Brighton Beach and moved to a dormitory that amounted to one big room that housed 20 people. I slept on one of many sofas and

Solidary shipping strike.

shared the bathroom with the others. There was little privacy and only a tiny storage area for my clothes and jewelry. Because of the number of people in the dormitory, a good night's sleep was next to impossible. I became depressed and missed my family more than ever, but I knew that I had to stay strong and reach my goal.

While I was living in the dormitory and commuting to Manhattan to attend English classes, I met a man who one day claimed that he knew me from Poland. When I inquired as to how he knew me, he told me that many years ago my former husband Andrew Soysal and this person's father worked on the same ship. What a small world. As we became better acquainted, this man, who was a few years younger and named Yanush, had a car and offered to drive me to English classes, which saved me considerable time and money.

Then one day during our commute, Yanush mentioned that he was having a difficult time paying for his expensive one-bedroom apartment in Bensonhurst, which is a large, multi-ethnic area in the borough of Brooklyn. Because the area had become stereotyped as a haven for Mafia members, it was known as a "Little Italy" of Brooklyn. In the late 1980s, the neighborhood had a large Italian-American population and was lined with small, Italian family-owned businesses— many of which had remained in the same family for several generations. Mob boss John Gotti's Ravenite Social Club was located in Little Italy at 247 Mulberry St, which is now a shoe store.

To help out, I offered to move in and share the monthly rent. Because his apartment had only one bedroom, he kept the bedroom and I slept in the living room. It was a workable arrangement for both of us. How little I knew at the time that Yanush's apartment would become a place where a major turning point in my life was about to take place.

In 1989, four thousand miles away in Poland things were suddenly looking up. Over time, the newly-formed, pro-democracy trade union "Solidarity" eroded the dominance of the communist led Polish United Workers Party. That year, the Solidarity candidate triumphed in Poland's first partially free and democratic elections since the end of World War II. This event heralded the collapse of the communist regime and the end to martial law.

CHAPTER SEVEN

RICHARD

One night when I was riding the subway, I closed my eyes and asked myself what exactly was I trying to accomplish in the United States? The answer that came to me was that in order to reach my goal to bring my family to America, I needed to earn a considerable amount of money—and that the only way I was going to accomplish that was to somehow acquire the help of influential people. It was then that a light went off. The way to meet these powerful, influential people in New York was to become a manicurist. What better way was there to meet these people than to actually be holding their hands while talking with them? Within a week of my epiphany, I enrolled in cosmetology school.

While I was attending cosmetology school and living with Yanush, I met a man named Richard Cantarella, who was a handsome Italian/American. Richard was a few years older and employed by the Coca-Cola Company. I first met Richard when he stopped by Yanush's apartment. At the time, because I was working nights, I was asleep on the sofa, and when Richard arrived, I quickly got up and went to the kitchen. As I was making coffee, I glanced into the living room where Richard and Yanush were talking. I felt an instant attraction to Richard, who later in the week invited Yanush and me to dinner. Upon learning that I was in cosmetology school, Richard asked me to do pedicures and manicures.

Weeks later, Yanush became interested in a girl who told him she felt uncomfortable coming to his apartment because I lived there. When Yanush told me I had to move, I began sleeping on the sofa at a friend's apartment. Her place was noisy and lacked privacy, but I had a roof over my head and an ocean view and remained optimistic.

Richard and I occasionally ran into each other at impromptu social gatherings, and he seemed to take a liking to me. He had been married, but his wife had died. She was Polish and they didn't have children.

One day Richard asked me where I was living, and when I told him that I was sleeping on a couch at a girlfriend's apartment, he asked me how much I was paying in rent.

"Two hundred dollars," I replied.

"How would you like to pay half that much and live in a house instead of an apartment and have your own bedroom?"

The home Richard was referring to belonged to him and was located in neighboring Rahway, New Jersey. The hundred dollars I would be saving in rent could easily pay for my train tickets to Manhattan. I accepted Richard's offer and moved into his three-bedroom home. Although the home wasn't a candidate for *Better Homes and Gardens* magazine, the house was comfortable and clean and had a nice backyard.

I was by no means excited over living in Rahway, which is a city in southern Union County, New Jersey, and considered part of metropolitan New York, being 25 miles from Manhattan. No one who lived there could tell me anything of significance about Rahway, which, following WWII suffered closures of most of its major manufacturing facilities (except for the pharmaceutical company Merck & Co.) and a general deterioration of the city's central business district.

Over the next few months, my relationship with Richard morphed from roommates to romance. Although up until now I had neither the time nor the interest in becoming involved in a serious relationship, Richard had many of the qualities that I admire in a man. Besides being hard working, because I respected and admired him on many levels, we became each other's helpmate.

Our relationship, however, did nothing to change two key realities—one, that my 90-day tourist visa had long since expired and, second, that my longing to be back with my family had become unbearable, the worst part being that my mother was calling constantly and begging me to come home, and it was heartbreaking to hear her crying. Succumbing to the mounting emotional pressure, I finally told Richard that I had decided to return to Poland.

Richard was not happy. "When will I see you?" he said forlornly.

"I don't know. My visa expired long ago, so I don't think I'll be able to get another visa for a long time, if ever."

"Then I'm coming to Poland to marry you."

Marrying Richard Cantarella at City Hall in Rahway.

Pope John Paul II with President Reagan.

Richard felt that if we were married that I'd have a far better chance of returning to the United States.

"No, you're not doing that because you have no time for vacation. You're a workaholic, and to get married to you in Poland takes a month, two months, three months. It's not simple like here."

"So then let's get married here," he said quickly.

"Married here?"

"Sure, why not?"

Although I wasn't entirely comfortable about getting married, Richard was so insistent that I eventually agreed. Two days later following our marriage before a Justice of the Peace, I returned to Poland, knowing that I may never again be allowed back into the United States.

My reunion with my children and parents was sheer bliss. We spent the first two days talking, singing, and laughing. I kept hugging them and simply wouldn't let go until someone pried us apart.

This was an ideal time to return to Poland. Because the United States had put pressure on the Soviet Union, the communists had softened their grip on Poland. Shortly before my arrival in Warsaw, in September 1987, Pope John Paul II and President Reagan met at a lavish mansion on Biscayne Bay in Miami where they created an informal alliance aimed at toppling the Soviet empire and ending communism once and for all.

Three months earlier in a landmark speech at the Berlin Wall, then-US President Ronald Reagan, standing at the Brandenburg Gate in front of two panes of bulletproof glass that protected him from potential snipers in East Berlin, had challenged Soviet Union leader Mikhail Gorbachev to "Tear down this wall!" which had become a symbol of communist oppression. As a footnote, two years and three months later in September 1990, President Reagan returned to Berlin, where he personally took a few symbolic hammer swings at a remnant of the Berlin Wall.

A month after I returned to Bialystok, Richard came to Po-

September 1990 President Reagan makes symbolic hammer swing at remnants of Berlin Wall.

land and we went to the American embassy where we filled out documents that were relevant to our marriage. When a week later I met privately with the lady at the American embassy and seemed reluctant to move forward with my case, she said, "Look, don't make our job difficult. If you don't want to go to the United States, then don't go. Tell me, tell him. Don't make a mess."

The problem I was having was that after I returned to Poland I realized how difficult life had been for me in the United States. In addition to having anything even resembling a safety net, there were many times that I felt discriminated against. Generally speaking, I think while in New York, I was repressing my insecure feelings and the harsh reality that I didn't feel at home. Perhaps this was simply because my family wasn't there. The root of my apprehension was difficult to pinpoint. Equally important was that I realized that I really didn't know Richard that well.

On the opposite side of the coin, the second reality was that even though the United States was gaining the upper hand on the Soviet Union, the oppressive conditions throughout Poland had only minimally subsided. As such, I recognized that I had little chance of a future in Poland. My farm was closed, which meant I'd have to start from scratch. Richard was leaving. My oldest daughter Jolanta wanted to attend dental school, and so I wanted to earn money to help pay her tuition. On the plus side, my younger daughter Anna agreed, although reluctantly, to return with me to the United States. Somewhere in the midst of my indecision, Richard had persuaded a Washington congressman to call the Polish authorities and strongly suggest that they approve my marriage to Richard and expedite my return to the United States. This congressman followed up his overseas telephone call with a formal letter.

Finally, because Richard had visited me several times in Poland, the American officials ruled that our marriage was legitimate and issued me a consulate passport. Along with Anna and a steel shipping container filled with our clothes and assorted belongings, I arrived back in the United States in the winter of

With Richard during his visit to Poland.

1989. Although Anna knew she would miss her friends and especially her big sister Jolanta, her spirits perked up when she realized how jealous her friends were that she was moving to America.

Two years earlier when I returned to Poland, Richard assured me that when I came back to the United States we would move from the mind-numbing city of Rahway to a more stimulating community closer to Manhattan. When Anna and I arrived from Poland, however, I learned that Richard had not moved from his house in Rahway and, furthermore, had little intention of doing so. In his mind, once Anna and I settled into family life, everything would be fine.

Besides being faced with living back in Rahway, I soon realized that Richard wanted me to be a housewife, which is a role I had always told Richard I had no interest in being. Besides the fact that I had been a successful businesswoman in Poland for many years and was determined to become established in a career when I came to New York two years earlier, I never wanted to risk ending up in a marriage like my mother's. I wanted to be independent and accomplish something in my life.

Anna's adjustment to living in the United States had its ups

With Richard Cantarella.

and downs. Initially, making friends was difficult for her because she didn't speak English. Even though her first school, which was located in the nearby town of Linden, was a Polish school, as strange as it was, nobody there spoke Polish. Moreover, because Richard didn't have experience with children, he tried to raise Anna the way he was raised by his father, which I didn't like. Few things are more disruptive to a family than parents who don't agree on how children should be raised. On the upside, it didn't take long for Anna to learn English, and she soon began to make friends. Also, I took her with me everywhere, which was fun for both of us.

For several months, Anna and I lived with Richard in Rahway, but our marriage soon deteriorated. Generally speaking, he simply didn't understand me, and at times was unnecessarily short with me and called Polish people stupid, which was hurtful. Although he always apologized, after a while his apologies meant nothing. Beside his increase of drinking alcohol, he began smoking incessantly. It seemed that I was constantly opening windows and emptying ashtrays. One day I said, "Stop it, you're going to get lung cancer."

"No," he protested. "I am King Kong."

"Yeah, you sound like King Kong up here," I replied sarcastically, pointing to his head, "because a normal person doesn't smoke like a chimney."

Eventually I saw no remedy to our ailing situation and divorced him, leaving with nothing more than what I brought to the marriage. Although Anna got along with Richard, who at times tended to spoil her, she was happy to leave as long as she was with me.

After leaving Rahway, I had little money for rent, so I moved with Anna to a small one-bedroom apartment in Linden, New Jersey. The unit was located in a two-story building. Our apartment was on the upper floor; the street level units were occupied by store owners on Main Street. The apartment was conveniently located a short distance from the train station and was also close to Anna's Catholic school. In addition to the cost of my train tickets to travel to and from work in New York, I had to pay for Anna's Catholic parochial school and her other needs. Sometimes I had only one dollar to eat and ended up buying a bag of popcorn that I ate on the evening train. One night I bought a pizza, and put it under my jacket to keep it warm because I wanted to share it with Anna when I got home. I was so happy to have her with me because, until I could arrange for my parents to come to America, Anna was the only family I had.

There were times when things became so difficult for Anna that she'd ask why we needed to stay in the United States and would point out that we still had our airline tickets with open return flights to Warsaw. When she would say things like this, I would fight back my tears. I had come to America at the age of

45 when many people were approaching retirement, and I was just starting on a new career with no guarantees of a future. But I had to see this through, whatever it took. My determination was so infectious that within ten minutes Anna would be back smiling with renewed hope.

A few weeks before leaving Rahway, I applied for a job at Elizabeth Arden's prestigious salon that was located in Manhattan. The woman who interviewed me, Mrs. Griffin, asked me to manicure her nails, and I thought she would kick me out when I was finished, I did such a terrible job (most likely because I was nervous). My saving grace was that after the manicure, I offered to give Mrs. Griffin a facial. While I was home in Poland, I read many books about facials and over time facials became one of my specialties. After I finished, Mrs. Griffin smiled and said, "I'll see you tomorrow."

I was excited to work for Elizabeth Arden because her company was a cosmetics empire in the United States. At the peak of her career, Elizabeth Arden was one of the wealthiest women in the world. In her salons and through her marketing campaigns, she stressed teaching women how to apply makeup, and pioneered such concepts as scientific formulation of cosmetics, beauty makeovers, and coordinating colors of eye, lip, and facial makeup. Miss Arden was largely responsible for establishing makeup as proper and appropriate—even necessary—for a ladylike image, when before makeup had often been associated with lower classes and such professions as prostitution. She targeted middle age and plain women for whom beauty products promised a youthful, beautiful image.

Anna and I lived in Linden, New Jersey until I moved to a bigger apartment in Bensonhurst so that I would be closer to work. Anna had a difficult time adjusting to living in this borough of Brooklyn. One day after school she got into a fight with four girls who thought she was snobby because she wore nice, simple clothes and no makeup or nail polish. At school these girls would call her a sissy and a snob, and punch her in

A picture taken in the backyard of Richard's home in Rahway, New Jersey.

the stomach. Over time, Anna remained resolute and eventually earned the girls' respect.

As was with me decades earlier when I was in school, Anna wasn't interested in boys, but was focused on trying to accomplish something with her life. Another way she followed in my footsteps was her love of music, particularly her love of the piano. When we lived in Bialystok under martial law, buying a piano was next to impossible, although I managed to purchase one. After practicing religiously for nearly a year, Anna had her first piano concert at age five. When Anna came with me to the United States, I had the piano shipped to Linden from Poland, much to Anna's (and our neighbors'!) delight.

I didn't work long for Elizabeth Arden because I couldn't tolerate many of their snotty clients who looked down on everyone. Often when I was doing their nails or giving them facials, they would lie on chaise lounges and talk about their money and material possessions, often making a point of gossiping about some person who was faced with financial ruin, was being investigated by the IRS, or was having an extramarital affair. When I would attempt to be cordial and polite, they would often talk down to me or turn up their noses. The worst ones were the gold-diggers.

One day I went to the manager, Mrs. Griffin, and told her I was leaving. She took my departure as a personal insult.

"What? You're leaving? Do you see those applications here on my table? They've been piling up for a year, and I hired you overnight, and now you tell me you're leaving?" She lit a cigarette, and then said, "Go home and sleep on it and come back tomorrow."

I didn't have to go home and sleep on anything. I purposely fanned her smoke from my face and replied, "There's no need. I already made my decision."

Back in my homeland country, Poland was finally on the rebound when on December 3, 1989, the Cold War officially ended when Soviet leader Mikhail Gorbachev met with US President George Bush aboard a Soviet ship docked at Malta's Marsaxlokk harbor. Three weeks earlier, Pope John Paul II, President Reagan, and Mikhail Gorbachev destroyed communism when, after increasing public unrest, East Germany finally opened the Berlin Wall. By the end of the year, official operations to dismantle the wall began. With the collapse of the Communist governments of Eastern Europe, historically the tearing down of the wall epitomized the final end of communism. Pope John Paul 11, who was elected by the second Papal conclave in October 1978, is recognized as helping end communist rule in his native Poland and eventually all of Europe.

CHAPTER EIGHT

THE HELMSLEY PALACE

Prior to leaving Elizabeth Arden, I interviewed for a manicurist opening at the Helmsley Palace Hotel and was hired on the spot because I was employed by Elizabeth Arden. The Helmsley Palace Hotel was unique because it combined the historic landmark Villard Mansion with a modern 55-story tower. Located at the center of Manhattan, the luxury hotel is directly across the street from St. Patrick's Cathedral.

Leona Helmsley was a New York City hotel operator and real estate investor who was born in New York and raised in Brooklyn. Together with her highly successful husband, Harry, their real estate fortune was estimated to be in excess of $5-billion. Part of their company's portfolio included the Empire State Building, the Helmsley Palace (now the New York Palace), the Park Lane Hotel, the Helmsley Middletown Hotel, the New York Helmsley Hotel (a.k.a. the New York Harley), the Helmsley Windsor Hotel, the St. Moritz (now the Ritz Carlton), the Carlton House hotels, the Harley Hotel chain, and the Helmsley Building.

When I began work at the Palace Hotel's salon "Eva of New York," my English was still not good, so I didn't talk much. Unlike my negative experience at Elizabeth Arden's, the clients who frequented the salon at the Palace Hotel were friendly towards me, most likely because the clients who frequented Eva of New York were well-established New Yorkers who had obtained their wealth from their own hard work.

One day the salon's manager sent me upstairs to do Leona Helmsley's nails. Everyone was convinced Mrs. Helmsley, who had a reputation for being difficult to get along with, would kick

Leona at work in her office.

me out. All I knew about the woman was that she was an extremely important person.

The moment I entered Mrs. Helmsley's office, it was readily apparent that Mrs. Helmsley lived large and was a busy person. Her office was well organized, elegant, meticulously clean, and adorned with expensive furniture and priceless artwork. Mrs. Helmsley's office was not part of her apartment that she maintained at the Palace Hotel. This office was strictly an office. In addition to maintaining a residence in this hotel, Leona and her husband maintained additional apartments in many of their other hotels, the most luxurious being at the Park Lane Hotel.

Five minutes after meeting Mrs. Helmsley, I found her to be a refreshing change from many of the snobbish gold-diggers I'd encountered at Elizabeth Arden's. She was beautiful, classy, flawlessly dressed, elegant, and to the point when she spoke. Her overall essence worked to perfection like an expensive Swiss watch.

The Helmsley Palace, "The only palace in
the world where the queen stands guard."

Leona and
Harry.

Leona was too smart to be a New York gold-digger and made her
first million on her own before her marriage to Harry Helmsley.
Mrs. Helmsley was a tough business woman who could instantly
judge a person in a matter of seconds just by observing their behavior, their mannerisms, and how they dressed. When she spoke,
her voice was both direct and commanding. She was the consummate rags to riches story, a classic example of an individual who
had the guts and determination to reach for the brass ring. Leona
Helmsley and my mother shared many of the same qualities.

Upon sizing me up, Leona appeared to accept me. I was
touched by her because she showed a sincere interest in me and
asked many questions. When I told her that I was from Bialystok,

she broke out with a huge smile because her father was born in Poland and had a store in Warsaw where he sold handbags. The more we talked the more we discovered that our families were much alike—most had come from humble beginnings, suffered considerable hardship, and learned the value of a dollar through years of hard work.

After I finished her nails and returned downstairs to the salon, I brought with me a standard slip of paper that noted the work I'd done and provided a space for Leona to include a tip. I handed the signed slip to the salon's manager, Hazel. Leona, however, had paid cash for my services and included a separate fifty dollar tip, which she personally placed in my coat pocket. I later found out that Leona rarely paid cash, and when she did it was because she wanted the person to feel special.

"Where's Mrs. Helmsley's check?" Hazel asked.

"I don't have a check. Mrs. Helmsley gave me 300 dollars in cash for services," I said as I handed her the money. Hazel was shocked that Leona hadn't given me the boot. I never told anyone how much of a tip Leona gave me, and after a while the other manicurists stopped asking.

After the first time I did Leona's nails, she would call down to the salon to make an appointment with me. Several of the other manicurists would tell her that I was booked, hoping they could be my replacement. Leona was no dummy and one day called and, after being told that I was booked for the day, said she wanted to speak with me directly. Moments later, a voice came over the salon's intercom, "Jolanta, line one, Leona Helmsley." You could hear a pin drop. The eyes of 50 customers and employees were suddenly riveted on me; Leona Helmsley had called to personally speak with me to make a private appointment. I was impressed by the reaction caused by the mere mention of Leona's name.

One day she asked me after I had finished with her manicure why I seemed to be in such a hurry.

"I need to go to Greenpoint to send some clothing to my mother in Poland," I replied.

"What size is she?" Leona asked.

"Well, she's about your size, Mrs. Helmsley, size eight or ten."

"If you don't mind, I have some clothes that I haven't worn and would fit your mother."

Had I heard correctly? Leona Helmsley wore clothing from the most expensive clothing lines in the world. For an instant I considered keeping the clothes myself, tucked away in my closet as a special treasure, and then in the next instant knew I would send them to my mother. "Are you sure?"

"Hubie?" Mrs. Helmsley called out to her assistant. "We need to get a package together and take it to the post office to send to Poland." Huberta "Hubie" Weyer, a Polish woman, had worked for Leona for many years and was totally devoted to her. Hubie was a classy woman, neat in appearance, and mindful to always dress down when at work so as not to upstage her boss.

"No, the post office is expensive," I interrupted. "I have a place that will send the package for one fourth the price of the post office."

Hubie's eyes darted at me. It was clear she was instantly alarmed by my suggesting that I had a better way of sending packages to Poland than did her boss, who no doubt had been sending packages to Poland for years. Leona looked at Hubie, and then back at me. "Okay," she said, smiling. She seemed to like the idea that even though I must have known that she was extremely wealthy, I was saving her money, even if only a few dollars.

One afternoon I was doing her nails and at one o'clock I gasped. When Leona asked what happened, I told her that it was exactly one year ago to the minute that I arrived back in the United States. "Let's celebrate," Leona announced. Suddenly beaming, she ordered two tall glasses of fresh-squeezed orange juice, with which we shared a toast.

That same day, she looked at me thoughtfully and said, "You know what? You're supposed to be in real estate." Having no idea what she meant by that, when I returned downstairs I looked up real estate in the dictionary. The following week, I told her that I had looked into getting into real estate and was shocked to learn that obtaining a real estate license would cost $1,000 and require me to spend considerable time studying for the state licensing exam.

"Money is not a problem if you have the time," Leona replied. When I told her I would gladly find the time, she told me to let her know when I had everything in order and that she would arrange for Hubie to write me a check. Mrs. Helmsley was the most generous person I've ever known.

Always a professional who used every resource at her disposal, one afternoon Leona asked me to give her a manicure while she interviewed a Polish couple she was considering for a position managing one of her hotels. Essentially, she wanted my assessment of the couple. To say that I was deeply touched that Leona Helmsley would want my opinion on anything having to do with her business would be a vast understatement.

Midway through the interview, I asked this couple a question in Polish (earlier Leona implied to the couple that she didn't speak Polish). Later, after the couple had left, she asked me why I'd done that, and I told her that I wanted to see if the couple would answer in Polish or English. If they answered in Polish, I would have advised Mrs. Helmsley to not hire them, the reason being that Mrs. Helmsley was the most important person in the room.

She smiled and said, "You bitch."

I smiled back and respectfully said, "You, too." By this time, I could joke with her in that manner because we had become friends.

After I'd been working for six months at Eva of New York, one of the cosmetologists, Stella, went on vacation and asked if I would temporarily take care of her clients, which I happily agreed to do. This top employee thought she was secure, but when she returned from vacation, she learned that the majority of her clients decided to change over to me.

EXECUTIVE OFFICE The Helmsley Building, 230 Park Avenue, New York, N.Y. 10169 212-679-3600

August 16, 1999

Ms. Jolanda Soysal
510 Main Street
#1324
New York, NY 10044

Dear Ms. Soysal:

I was delighted to receive your birthday greeting card. What a lovely surprise!

Thank you for keeping me in your thoughts and for remembering my special day with your nice gesture.

Your warm wishes were appreciated and brought added joy to my birthday.

Sincerely,

Leona M. Helmsley

/hbw

NEW YORK

The Helmsley Carlton House
660 Madison Avenue
New York, N.Y. 10021
212/838-3000

The Helmsley Middletowne
148 East 48th Street
New York, N.Y. 10017
212/755-3000

800-221-4982

ABOVE: Letter thanking me for condolences following the death of her husband. LEFT: Leona in 2009 with her beloved Maltese "Trouble."

Stella came where I was working and said pointedly, "I'm back from vacation."

"Yes, Stella, I know that," I responded matter-of-factly, suggesting that I gave no importance to her statement. Without warning, she viciously slapped my face. It took all I had in my power to remain calm. I went to the bathroom and washed my reddened face. After redoing my makeup, I returned to the salon and acted like nothing had happened, although my look and demeanor conveyed a different story. Stella was afraid of me for five months and visibly shook whenever I came near her.

Mr. Samuel Alper, who was a steady client, owned a diamond business at 48th Street and 5th Avenue and was friends with singing heartthrob Frank Sinatra. He was a nice man who enjoyed hearing my broken English, my opinions on any subject he raised, and was particularly amused by my naivety. One afternoon while I was doing his nails, he said, "Jolanta, I have an extra ticket to see Frank Sinatra tonight. Would you care to come? Frank's a personal friend of mine."

I continued buffing his nails and replied nonchalantly, "I'm sorry, perhaps another time. I'm doing something with my daughter."

A nearby hairdresser looked at me and remarked, "Jolanta, are you okay? I mean, did you hear—"

"Why do you say that?" I interrupted.

"Frank Sinatra—*the* Frank Sinatra." She didn't understand that even though Frank Sinatra has always been well known throughout Poland, I had a zero social life.

Several months into my employment at Eva of New York, one of the salon's clients, Mrs. Hideko, invited me to have lunch with her in the Plaza Hotel Oak Room. During lunch she told me about her company's new line of beauty machines and offered me a temporary job as a pitch woman, which I accepted. If things worked out well, the temporary job potentially could result in fulltime employment as a company representative.

During my first show in City Center, I was onstage demonstrating how the machine worked, having been given only a brief explanation about its operation. Because I had inadvertently failed to cover the sink where the machine's water drained under considerable pressure, when the drain cycle clicked in, water went flying in all directions, nearly flooding the stage and getting water on the first two rows of the audience. As company reps quickly covered the sink, I hardly knew what to say, so I simply pointed out that this waterfall is what happens when a dumb blonde fails to follow the machine's simple instructions. To my surprise, the audience erupted with laughter and applause.

This embarrassing geyser wasn't my only fatal mistake. I made several more errors during my four day tour. In a sense, my sales pitch began to resemble a cross between a Groucho Marx stand-up routine and a Three Stooges bit. As my last show came to an end, Mrs. Hideko thanked me and told me I could go. I had the feeling that she was happy to be seeing the last of me, although I was looking forward to receiving her company's check for $1,500, which was our agreed upon compensation. Three days later, the check arrived. When I opened the envelope, I was shocked and surprised to see the amount was for $3,000, twice what we had agreed upon. Thinking the company's accounting department had made a mistake, I called the company and was put through directly to Mrs. Hideko.

"Hello, Jolanta. I was expecting your call." As things turned out, my comical personality overshadowed my weak sales pitch, enough so that her company had received three times the orders Mrs. Hideko had expected. As a result, she wanted me to work for her fulltime and go on a tour of the United States and Canada pitching her beauty machines. As financially attractive as her offer was, the job simply wasn't for me because it lacked the personal one-on-one relationship with my individual clients that I had come to love.

Chaucer's venerable proverb "All good things must come to an end" inevitably became true of my work at Eva of New York. Apparently the manager felt that I spent too much time upstairs with Leona Helmsley. One day it was pouring rain outside and the salon was empty. Leona called and wanted a manicure and pedicure, so I went upstairs and ended up staying with her for five hours. When I returned, I gave Hazel 700 dollars in cash from Mrs. Helmsley. Instead of being thankful, the manager was furious. "Where were you?" Hazel roared. "Your client has been waiting two hours for you."

"Waiting for me? There's another three manicurists over there and she wants me? She didn't have an appointment. I brought 700 dollars for you."

"I don't care about your money."

"This isn't my money. I made it for your salon."

"And how much did *you* make?"

I didn't care for the sudden smirk on Hazel's face and my tone said as much. "That's not your business."

The woman's eyes widened with authority. "Really? Fine. You're fired. You have to leave in a week."

Much to her surprise, I thanked her and walked away. The

Harry Helmsley mausoleum.

reason I didn't mind being terminated was because I had another job lined up, which Hazel probably figured out. If I were to stay another week, this would give me time to talk with my clients, most of whom I might take with me to my new job. Moments later, Hazel walked over to my station and said, "Leave now."

After leaving the salon at Leona Helmsley's Palace Hotel, I kept in touch with Leona for many years. She died in 2007 at the age of 87 and was entombed at Sleep Hollow Cemetery beside her husband Harry, who died in 1997 at the age of 88. Her passing and funeral were tearful days for me.

CHAPTER NINE

HARMONIE CLUB

I was truly excited over having landed a job at the renowned Harmonie Club. Located at 5th Avenue and 61st Street, the Harmonie Club was a closed club and the oldest private Jewish club in the world. Its founders envisioned a fraternity bound together by mutual social interests, the chief of which at that time were song recitals. Initially, German descent was a requirement for membership or employment. The club had a basement bowling alley, bedrooms on the upper floors, overseas jaunts to St. Moritz, candlelight suppers on Sunday nights, waiters in white gloves carrying hot bread and relish trays, and golf tournaments.

I began working there in 1991 and soon became bored with its geriatric clients (many of whom were 25 cent tippers) and my $90-$200 per week salary that was based on commissions. After two weeks, I decided to leave. I went to the manager, who in the interest of my staying offered me a raise to a guaranteed $600 per week. The increase was enough to convince me to stay, and working conditions improved. To my delight, when many of the clients who were Polish Jews learned that I was Polish, my tips gradually increased from 25 cents to as high as 20 dollars!

Drawing on my childhood entrepreneurial roots and following the lead of Elizabeth Arden, to supplement my income, I made my own cosmetics, specifically lotions made fresh every day. Before I reported for work at the Harmonie Club at nine o'clock, I made $200 selling my cosmetics. Several of my best sellers were made from special cosmetics formulas given to me by my grandmother Emily.

ABOVE: Leon Hess addressing New York Jets media.
BELOW: Hess gas station in New York.

After my first month, the salon's manager told me that the most important member of the club was coming in that day. In my travels around New York, I had noticed signs on many gas stations that read "HESS." And so on Thursday, *the* Mr. Hess arrived for his scheduled nail appointment with me.

Leon Hess, at 75 years of age, was the kindest gentleman I ever met. He was born into a Jewish family in Asbury Park, New Jersey. His father was a kosher butcher who emigrated from Lithuania and—after arriving in the United States—worked as an oil delivery man in Asbury Park. Leon Hess worked as a driver for his father's company, and after the company went bankrupt in 1933 during the Great Depression, Leon reorganized the company. In the late 1950s he built his first refinery, and in 1960 he opened a chain of gas stations. In 1969, Mr. Hess acquired the Amerada Petroleum Corporation, one of the largest producers of crude oil in the United States. In 1947, he married Norma Wilentz who was also Jewish. Norma's father was the former Attorney General David T. Wilentz who prosecuted Bruno Richard Hauptmann in the famous Lindbergh baby kidnapping case.

Quiet and classy, Mr. Hess liked me because I'm a family person. Whenever he came in, he asked about my mother, who was my favorite subject. Thankfully there were never any life-threatening emergencies involving my mother in Poland. Had she become seriously ill and died without my being with her, I could have never forgiven myself.

I enjoyed joking with Mr. Hess so much that, to accommodate his busy schedule, I sometimes opened the salon on Sundays. It was during one of these Sundays that Mr. Hess first met Anna, who came to work with me. He instantly fell in love with her. Later, Anna would come to the club to help during special occasions and private parties. The club had separate coatrooms for men and women. Anna would be working in the women's coatroom and suddenly look up to discover that Mr. Hess had gone out of his way to come visit her and would give her a big kiss on her cheek. For a long time, many of the salon's employees were jealous of the attention the salon's most prized client paid to Anna. Needless to say, Anna was overjoyed.

At that time, my daughter Jolanta had graduated dental school and was now enrolled in medical school in Poland, and Anna was here with me. Anna continued working at the Harmonie Club after school. She was attending school in Bensonhurst. After six months, she'd saved $3,000, which she sent to her big sister to help purchase a condominium. One of the employees at the Harmonie Club got upset because Anna was working without belonging to the union and was only 14 years of age. The manager didn't know how to let her go because he knew that Mr. Hess adored Anna. Months earlier, Mr. Hess said to Anna, "You're my granddaughter," and kissed her on the cheek in front of the salon's manager. It didn't matter. The manager had no choice but to let Anna go.

One of Mr. Hess's biggest holdings was that he owned the NFL's New York Jets. He bought the football team when it had been in a slump. Years later, Mr. Hess lured then-disgruntled New England Patriots head coach Bill Parcells to New York in 1997. Parcells led the team back to relevance and coached them to the AFC Championship Game in 1998.

From the day Mr. Hess acquired ownership of the team, he was a huge supporter. With rare exception, after every home game, win or lose, he ate at Lusardi's, which was a Northern Italian restaurant located on the Upper East Side of Manhattan.

Mr. Hess had a great sense of humor. One day he brought his wife Norma to my workplace because they were having lunch in the hotel. With a totally straight face, he introduced me to her as his girlfriend, which caused me to immediately turn red. His wife seemed to stare at me for the longest time, and then she finally smiled and commented, "My husband has good taste." They both laughed. Clearly his wife was used to this old

Anna at age 16 working at the Harmonie Club.

gag of her husband's. It took me a few moments to join in the laughter and a few more moments for my face to return to its natural color.

As was the case with my mother, Mr. Hess was always ready to help anyone in dire need. He was loyal to those who worked for him. One of those people was his barber who had cut Mr. Hess's hair for many years. This man worked at home and Mr. Hess was his only client. When this barber's son and daughter-in-law died in a car accident, Mr. Hess offered to help care for their two children, in a sense unofficially becoming their god-parent.

One day Mr. Hess arrived at the Harmonie Club with blue hair that was so noticeable that it was shocking. "What happened to you?" I asked. "I think you need to change barbers."

"Accidents happen," Mr. Hess replied. "Nick put too much rinse on or something. Anyway, Nick is the best barber in the world and I'm with him to the end." He then told me about the progress Nick was making with his orphaned grandchildren. What a great story about Mr. Hess and his barber. As a footnote, Mr. Hess walked around for a week with that blue hair.

Another example of Mr. Hess's care and generosity began when in November 1992, one of the New York Jets players— Dennis Byrd—suffered a spinal cord injury during an NFL game against the Kansas City Chiefs that left him unable to walk. Mr. Hess was devastated and visited his injured player every day at the hospital. Thankfully, after extensive physical therapy, Dennis Byrd was able to walk again, although he never returned to playing football.

Mr. Hess had a wall around him because he was a private person who purposely isolated himself. When somebody would arrive at the salon, he would close his eyes and then open them slowly to check to make sure the person had left. He didn't want to talk to anybody, so he pretended like he was asleep in the chair. He jokingly allowed me to be on the short list of people he allowed into his personal space. I think he did this because he knew that I had no interest in his, or anyone else's, money. Aware that I had a personal friendship with Leona Helmsley and other millionaires, one day Mr. Hess told Anna, "Your mother doesn't need me because she knows so many powerful people."

Not long after Mr. Hess and I had become friends, he learned that my mother was tentatively planning on traveling to New York for a visit. When Mr. Hess learned of this, he asked what plans I had with regards to showing my mother around the Big Apple. When I told him I didn't have any plans, he said, "Bad, bad daughter!"

"No—bad, bad knee."

Sorrowfully, my mother suffered from severe arthritis in her knee, which made it extremely difficult for her to get around. Upon hearing this, Mr. Hess wrote down the contact information for the best New York surgeon who specializes in knee replacements and said that he would personally call this doctor and advise him that I would be contacting him.

One personality trait that I noticed in many wealthy people was their flare for becoming joyously obsessed over the smallest of things. I suppose when a person has enough money to last ten lifetimes they can devote their time and energy to whatever might tickle their fancy. Mr. Hess was no exception, as is illustrated by the following story.

At Christmas time, Mr. Hess asked what I was serving for Christmas dinner.

"What do you mean? Whatever I get."

"No, not whatever you get. You must have a traditional goose."

"Goose is traditional?" I said.

"Absolutely. Although it was a prized turkey that Scrooge sent that urchin to buy at the end of *A Christmas Carol*, a goose was the original centerpiece on Cratchit's menu."

"I didn't know that."

"It's true. While most American families this Christmas will sit down to meal of turkey or ham or beef this Christmas, goose is the traditional Christmas meat—and has been long before Dickens wrote about its succulence!"

I couldn't help but return Mr. Hess's proud smile, after which he asked, "Do you like goose?"

"Who doesn't? Hmmmm?" I replied, sliding my tongue over my lips.

"I have a goose every year," he announced. "So buy a goose."

The next day when I heard from Mr. Hess, he asked if I'd bought a goose.

"No, I haven't."

"I already figured that out. You spent too much money on cosmetics, right?"

Well, he was partially correct. I had tried to find a goose, and discovered they were by no means in large supply. I also concluded that if and when I did find one, the price would be considerably more than turkey.

"No," I answered while stifling a laugh. "I'm still looking."

I eventually did find a goose and served it that Christmas for dinner. In the years that followed, in honor of Mr. Hess, I've often served goose and lovingly recalled this particular obsession of his in his search for Scrooge's prized "succulent meat."

When it came to my newly-formed relationship with people I met in America, generally speaking, I got along with all people. Where the difference often arose was that I seemed to get along better and more easily with wealthy people because since childhood I had a strong aversion toward people who are rude. Because of the circles wealthy people run in, they almost always are more polite and better mannered than many people I met who were poor. In addition, I related more to the work ethic of people of wealth, most of whom worked hard like my mother, while many of the poor people I met in America had the same sense of entitlement as my father had.

I spent most of my free time at the Harmonie Club studying English and American history. I studied American history because I knew that one day I would be taking a written test for my American citizenship. One afternoon a distinguished looking gentleman who had been coming to the salon noticed me studying. After introducing himself as Geoffrey and learning that I was studying American history, he took my notebook that was thick with multiple choice questions and answers and asked if he could quiz me.

"Sure," I replied.

He pulled up a chair and over the next 20 minutes ran me through more than 100 questions, all of which I gave the correct answer. He was so impressed that he gave me his card and said that if I ever needed help to feel free to call him. Hours later when I finished work, I walked into the hotel lobby where I found him waiting for me. After greeting me, he asked if I would join him for dinner, which I accepted.

When we walked out of the English school, he walked me to his awaiting limousine, where his chauffeur opened the rear door. As we stepped into the limo, I heard several people say in a loud whisper, "Oh, my god, that's Mr. Schrader."

I was soon to find out that Geoffrey Schrader was as rich as Mr. Hess. When Mr. Schrader asked me where I'd like to have dinner, because we were close to Chinatown, I said I'd love Chinese food.

Twenty minutes later we arrived at an exclusive Chinese restaurant that was located on the wharf. Not surprisingly, our dinner was magnificent. I kept asking him what he did for a living, and he kept giving me vague responses. Finally, asked me if I'd like to see where he worked.

"It's eleven o'clock at night," I replied.

"And the start of my work day. Come, I'll take you there."

Fifteen minutes later, his limousine drove along Park Avenue and finally eased up to a high-rise office building opposite the famed Waldorf Astoria Hotel. We entered the building's stunning lobby and as we rode the elevator to the 12th floor, I thought *what kind of office could be open at midnight?* Moments later Mr. Schrader opened the door to his office, which amounted to an enormous room filled with people sitting at computers and standing in front of huge projection screens and talking on telephones.

"What are you doing here?" I asked with amazement.

"I'm an international lawyer, and it's now five o'clock in the morning in Paris and in London."

Over the next several months we met for dinner when time permitted. Although his business was more far-reaching than mine, considering that I also had Anna to care for, I had as much difficulty finding free time as did Mr. Schrader. After two years, I was surprised when one evening over dinner he asked me if I had any financial problems.

"Me? No, not really. Why do you ask?"

I guess he was surprised by my answer because he felt that maybe I was seeing him because of his wealth and was looking for a long term, committed relationship. Then one night as we were leaving a Broadway show, he casually asked me, "What do you think about changing your last name?"

Much to my surprise, and perhaps even to his, his question scared me, and I soon stopped seeing him. For some time I had begun to feel the same way I did years earlier about my Italian friend Giovanni Ferrara. Mr. Schrader was so rich and constantly traveling to his offices in Europe that his lifestyle made me feel like a nobody.

Over the next six months, I received scores of messages from him on my answering machine, none of which I returned. Finally, he wrote a letter, asking me what happened and said that if I was uncomfortable living in New York that he was inviting me to Bel Air in Southern California where he had a residence. It's true that he made me feel special and that he was a handsome and extremely nice man who would be a dream come true for any smart woman. But I got scared. I once went to lunch with him at the Yale Club where I overhead a lady who was having lunch with a group of women ask in a loud whisper, "Who is she?"

I pretended I didn't hear what she said, but it hurt me. What was wrong with my having lunch at the Yale Club? Did I not belong there? And if for whatever that reason was, would this result in my constantly hearing this all the time whenever I was being escorted somewhere by Mr. Schrader?

I guess this boils down to the biggest problem I faced over and over again when I first came to the United States— discrimination. Whether they intentionally meant to or not, many people made me feel like I didn't belong in America and would often allude to this by asking me where I was from.

"From China," I would reply sarcastically. "What difference does it make where I'm from? Where are YOU from?" and before they could answer I'd walk away because their cheap comment upset me.

Even after I'd been a resident in the United States for many years, I still felt like a foreigner. The discrimination wasn't racial. It was that I felt like an outsider from Europe—and not from the glamorous parts of Europe like Italy, France, and Spain—but from Poland, which Americans identified with being part of the Soviet Union—a communist country.

Of course, there were people in America who treated me in a totally opposite manner. Although a bit of a mystery to me, much to my delight was the fact that many of the wealthy people I met were drawn to me and wanted to help me succeed in life. One such example was a charming French woman named Lucy Cassel. She was from a well-established old money family in Europe and maintained an apartment at the Park Avenue Hotel, although her primary residence was a beautiful home in Paris.

Mrs. Cassel's husband was a regular member of the Harmonie Club, and over a period of time his wife took a sincere interest in me and Anna. After knowing us for a month, she one day offered to take Anna and me shopping at Bloomingdale's, which at that time was a high-end store in New York. Because she was eager to spend time with us, we agreed to go with her. Not long after we arrived at Bloomingdale's, Mrs. Cassel told Anna and me to buy whatever we wanted, and I had no doubt that the sky was the limit. I thanked her and added that we really have everything we need. Throughout my life, I've been happier when I give than when I receive.

Then one cold, icy morning she came to the salon and wanted to discuss adopting us. While I was deeply touched by her offer, I told her that I already had a mother, who was also Anna's grandmother, and that our being adopted by anyone outside our family would be painful for my mother—and me. Mrs. Cassel explained that adopting me was a business matter that somehow had to do with her leaving me money in her will without having to pay taxes. She and her husband were getting up in years and had no children or close family members. She was an extremely nice lady, but I didn't want her money. I couldn't agree to this adoption because it would be too stressful for my mother—and me.

Unfortunately, my final parting with Mrs. Cassel was both awkward and unpleasant. One afternoon she appeared at the same time as did Mr. Hess. I was the only manicurist working, and somehow there was a mix-up that resulted in appointments being made at the same time for Mrs. Cassel and Mr. Hess.

Although Mrs. Cassel was a member of Elizabeth Arden and not a member of the Harmonie Club, which was an exclusive men's club, she nonetheless requested that I give her a manicure. The problem was that I was scheduled to give a manicure to Mr. Hess, who intervened and offered to give Mrs. Cassel his appointment and that he could come back the next day.

Besides having become a close friend, Mr. Hess was the number one client of the Harmonie Club. "No, no," I said, then turned

Ready for work.

to Mrs. Cassel. "I'm sorry, Mrs. Cassel, I didn't know that you had an appointment at the same time as Mr. Hess."

She looked at me without words, clearly hurt by my decision. After Mrs. Cassel left, Mr. Hess said, "You should have taken Mrs. Cassel. I would have waited."

"No, no, you're number one, Mr. Hess. Everyone else is behind you—and you have a beautiful laugh like Marlene Dietrich."

He broke out into that infectious laugh of his and began tickling me. We were making such a ruckus that I had to close the doors that opened into the hotel's interior. Sadly, I never saw or heard from Mrs. Cassel again.

Later, when I looked into this matter of Mrs. Cassel and Mr. Hess having appointments with me at the same time, it turned out that a particular barber had purposely scheduled two appointments so as to cause me this embarrassing problem. Earlier that month, I had gotten into a fight with the same barber who called me a lesbian because I didn't have a boyfriend.

I said, "I have more responsibility helping to care for my parents and daughters. I don't have time for hanky-panky."

Besides calling me a lesbian, he sexually abused me when one afternoon he walked close to me and pushed his groin into my elbow. In response, I punched him against a wall, and he crumbled to the floor. I then gathered up my things and left.

I was afraid because this barber was Italian, and he had often made comments about having ties to the Italian mafia. I didn't want to risk the deaths of me and my daughter over a manicurist job—or any job for that matter—so I didn't speak to strangers on the street for a long time because I suspected these people might be mafia hitmen. Many of the club's powerful clients, including Mr. Hess, came to my defense, as well as the owner, who offered me more money and a better chair. But I just couldn't take that barber any longer and ultimately left the Harmonie Club.

After separating from Richard Cantarella and waiting our divorce to become final, I remained hopeful that the paperwork for my green card would soon be finalized. After several more months elapsed, my sister Alicja called from London and asked how my green card was coming along. When I said I didn't know, she told me that I needed to gather all my paperwork and personally go to the immigration office.

Later that week, I arrived at the immigration office in New York. The lady across the counter looked up my case status on her computer, then leaned forward and whispered to me, "Get out of here because according to your case file, you're supposed to be arrested because you're now illegally in the United States."

When I tried to explain that I had an attorney working on my case, she reiterated that I needed to leave or she would have no choice but to have me arrested. In the week that followed, much to my horror, I discovered that the Polish attorney I had retained took my money and did nothing. I had been working at Elizabeth Arden, Eva of New York, and now the Harmonie Club without a green card or social security number because my employers were under the impression that my paperwork was in its final stages of being processed and would soon be forthcoming.

The following day I was doing a manicure for a powerful businesswoman whom I liked very much. She said, "Jolanta, why are you so quiet? Are you not feeling well?"

"No, it's much worse," I said. After I told her what had happened at the immigration office, she assured me that everything was going to be all right and asked me to call her secretary. Within a couple of days, this woman had arranged for me to speak with a powerful New York immigration attorney. When I met with him, he ended our meeting by saying, "Go to the immigration office in Brooklyn, and if they don't want to talk to you, give them my card and tell them that I personally represent you."

The next day, I arrived at the immigration office in Brooklyn and had a two hour interview with a man named Tony Avento, who spent several hours researching my case. When he was finished, he told me that he couldn't promise me that I would be receiving a green card. Two weeks went by and then one afternoon a card came in the mail from the immigration office, except it wasn't green. When Anna arrived home from school, she looked at the card and said, "You got your green card!"

"What green card?" I replied.

The problem was that the green card was pink instead of

green. This was because in 1989, in an attempt to stay one step ahead of counterfeiters, the INS changed the green card to a peach-colored card.

Anna started jumping up and down in celebration. I called Tony Avento and told him I wanted to take him to dinner at his favorite Italian restaurant. He accepted my invitation and asked if he could bring his girlfriend, to which I happily agreed.

"I'll drive," he said. "Where should I pick you up?"

"I'm working at the Harmonie Club in Manhattan."

After a long pause, he said, "Without a green card?"

"What? Who told you that? I have a green card right here in my hand!"

We went to dinner, and he asked me about my life in Poland. I told him the story about Mr. Schreiber because it made people laugh. When dinner ended, I said, "Let's have an after dinner drink to celebrate my getting a green card."

"Too soon to celebrate."

"Why?"

"We should celebrate when you become an American citizen."

CHAPTER TEN

VICTOR

I was fortunate to have worked at some of the finest hotels in New York. The 47-story Waldorf Astoria Hotel is one of the world's most prestigious and best known hotels. Several of the luxury suites are named after luminaries who lived or stayed in them such as the Cole Porter Suite, the Royal Suite (named after the Duke and Duchess of Windsor), the MacArthur Suite, and the Churchill Suite. Herbert Hoover lived there from his retirement for over 30 years, and Frank Sinatra kept a suite at the Waldorf from 1979 until 1988.

Manhattan's 41-story Pierre Hotel rose forty-one stories that allowed for unrestricted views of Central Park. Modeled after Mansart's Royal Chapel at Versailles, its topmost floors rendered it an easily recognizable landmark on the New York skyline.

In September 1991, the St. Regis Hotel had been renovated at a cost of over $100-million into one of the most luxurious hotels in the world. The hotel has always had a number of permanent residents, as well as transient guests. Throughout the 1960s and 1970s, the artist Salvador Dalí lived at the hotel every fall and winter, and Marlene Dietrich maintained an apartment there. The Beatles John Lennon made a demo of "Happy Christmas War Is Over" in his room at the St. Regis.

After I left the Harmonie Club, I got a job at the St. Regis Hotel that had a salon that was put together by Sal Fodera who had won many internationals awards for men's haircutting. "Salon Fodera" was the kind of barbershop, full of leather, brass and marble that existed in the bygone days when men wore gray felt hats and women wore white gloves. At the door, customers traded

RIGHT:
Sal Fodera
Salon. BELOW:
Sal Fodera (left)
with me and
Regis Philbin.

their cares for a cup of coffee or a glass of wine before slipping into a leather chair studded with gold tacks. Among Mr. Fodera's customers was Hollywood's legendary leading man Cary Grant.

I answered a *New York Times* manicurist wanted ad that was placed by Sal Fodera. The salon was going to open soon and was planning a grand opening. When I met with Mr. Fodera, the manager of the rapturously beautiful Liz Taylor (at that time Mrs. Larry Fortensky) walked into the salon. After the two exchanged greeting, Mr. Fodera introduced me asked, "So what do you think of this lady?"

Liz Taylor's manager smiled and replied, "Wow, she'd be a nice addition. I'll be her first client!"

Mr. Fodera turned to me and said, "I'm going to hire you, but I already hired someone two weeks ago and I'll have to fire her."

I felt terrible that hiring me meant that the other manicurist who was hired two weeks earlier would now be fired without having even spent one day at work. No doubt she was excited about working for this new salon that had become the talk of the town.

Several days before the salon's opening, I was at the salon putting together my manicurist supplies. I was eating lunch with a few other employees in the coatroom and asking general questions about the salon. An older Spanish lady named Nuri walked into the coatroom and after listening my casual questioning, said to me in an unfriendly tone, "Don't ask me about anything. I'm not going to help you."

Because manicurists make the majority of their income based on their ability to obtain clients, much of which is done through word-of-mouth, many manicurists keep their methods to themselves. Moreover, the woman probably didn't like my accent. Having spent considerable time with Leona Helmsley, who was dubbed by some as the "Queen of Mean" because of her no-nonsense approach to dealing with rudeness, I answered Nuri directly. "Of course I won't ask you because you're stupid."

The woman gasped as her eyes widened. Moments later, she quickly left the coatroom. I wasn't done with her.

That weekend we had the grand opening. I wore a Christian Dior suit, did my hair and makeup, and was ready to "rock and roll," which was a common phrase of that era. Salon Fodera was a small shop, but within a few hours we had 800 esteemed guests. A gentleman who was one of the guests of honor asked me to dance, and for 15 minutes we danced all over the salon. The festivities were exhilarating and I wished that my family were present to partake in the joy.

Later, when I was sitting sipping champagne, Nuri came to me and said in a meek voice, "You know, Jolanta, on the outside I look like a bad person, but on the inside I'm actually very nice."

I smiled warmly, took a sip of champagne, and then replied, "That's wonderful to hear, Nuri, and it's interesting that you mention this because—well, I look nice on the outside, but on the inside I'm a real bitch."

Once again, the woman gasped as her eyes widened, then she quickly turned and walked off. Unfortunately, this wasn't the last time I was to cross swords with this woman.

One of several exciting aspects of working as a manicurist in New York's top salons, most of which were located in the city's best hotels, was that I was forever meeting famous people from all walks of life and from every part of the globe. One example is Jordan's King Hussein bin Talal whose rule extended through the Cold War and four decades of Arab–Israeli conflict. He was one of the longest-serving leaders in international politics.

When I was working at Sal Fodera's salon, King Hussein traveled to the United States for cancer treatment and stayed at the Regency Hotel. Twice he brought his entire immediate family who took over the entire tenth floor of the hotel.

The first time I arrived on the tenth floor with my manicurist cart, I was instantly overwhelmed by the sight of what looked like a platoon of stern-faced armed security guards. I tried to back into the elevator when one security guard, who must have

Broadway star Elaine Stritch was a frequent customer—when she was in town.

New York Giants NFL star Frank Gifford.

Grand opening Fodera's Salon.

recognized my cart and smock, yelled, "Madame! Madame! Stop! You're in the right place!"

For several months, I took care of King Hussein twice a week. The first time I worked on his wife, she asked me how much money went in my pocket. "Whatever a client gives me as a tip. After six o'clock in the evening, I can work privately." From that moment, she never made an appointment with me before six o'clock.

At that time, Anna and I were living in Bensonhurst, Brooklyn. I had to be up at four in the morning to fix breakfast for Anna, prepare her clothes and get her off to school, then travel to Manhattan for work. One evening after I finished with the King's family around eleven o'clock, the King invited me to have dinner with his Royal Family, but because my daughter Anna was at home and expecting me, I politely declined the king's invitation.

Later, when I was riding home on the subway, I reflected on what I'd done and started laughing. A lady sitting beside me asked why I was laughing, and when I told her that I'd turned down a dinner invitation from Jordan's King Hussein, she also started laughing. Before long, the story spread throughout the subway car and everyone was laughing.

On my second day working at Sal Fedora's, I was sweeping the floor because Mr. Fedora insisted the salon had to look like a million dollar piece of jewelry. So when I wasn't doing manicures, my client was a broom. The manager walked up to me and said that someone wanted to speak with me and indicated a distinguished looking, tall, slim, gray-haired man. I walked over to where Mr. Victor Potamkin was getting a haircut and introduced myself. Now that I was much closer, I couldn't help but notice that he had a genuine smile and hoarse voice of Jack Klugman, the twinkling eyes of George Burns, and the physique of Victor Mature.

Mr. Potamkin showed me his hands and asked if I could do something with his nails.

"Sure." I sat down and began manicuring his nails.

Mr. Potamkin never took his eyes off me and finally asked, "Where are you from?"

"I'm from Poland."

"Don't tell me you're from Bialystok," he said politely.

I thought, *oh, my goodness, he knows me.* How many rich people from Poland are now living in New York? "Yes," I replied.

"My mother was born in Bialystok!" he proudly announced, then got up from the chair, gave me a strong hug and whispered in my ear, "One day I'm going to steal you away from here."

He broke away from me and playfully winked his eye.

I said, "Why not today?"

We laughed as he sat back down.

I would later learn that Victor Potamkin was initially drawn to me because I so closely resembled his wife Luba to whom he was still happily married and madly in love. Tragically, Luba had been bedridden for 15 years with Alzheimer's. She was presently living at their home in Miami with 24-hour nursing care. Victor

ABOVE: Victor wearing his signature glasses. LEFT: Potamkin Cadillac T-shirt.

Luba Potamkin.

Luba at Diabetes
charity.

Victor with President Reagan.

To Victor Potamkin
With best wishes,
Ronald Reagan

took care of her every day because he knew she liked to look beautiful. So every day her caretaker dressed her, manicured her nails, and did her hair and makeup. Even though Luba was in the final stages of Alzheimer's and often incoherent, he did this for her because he was a wonderful, caring husband.

We talked throughout his manicure and I learned that Victor Potamkin had been born in 1912 to a Polish/Russian family and had three brothers and a sister. As a young man, he drove a truck for his father's fish market at 4th and Christian Streets, then peddled cut chickens in Camden.

Eventually he became a supercharged car salesman who turned an ailing Manhattan Cadillac agency into the flagship of a $1-billion-a-year automotive empire. Although born and raised in Philadelphia, Mr. Potamkin was a consummate New Yorker who rubbed shoulders with corporate titans like Lee Iacocca and

William Levitt, President Ronald Reagan, mayors of Philadelphia and New York, and judges on the federal and state benches. He was a master showman and salesman who kept gold Cross pens in his desk drawer that said, "STOLEN FROM VIC POTAMKIN" and once passed out one-dollar bills in New York that had his picture pasted over George Washington's. The bucks were encased in plastic printed with the slogan, "Betcha a buck you can't beat our deal! Vic Potamkin."

When I finished manicuring Mr. Potamkin's nails, he stood and slipped a tip into my coat pocket. One of the ladies who previously did Mr. Potamkin's nails implied that he was a modest tipper and told me I was welcome to him. I removed the bill Mr. Potamkin had placed in my coat pocket and said, "Let's check." Mr. Potamkin had given me a $100 tip (in 2015 equal to $175).

The woman's mouth dropped open. "What did you do for him?!" she said loudly.

What a silly question. From that point on, Mr. Potamkin became my client. He was one of the big tippers in the salon.

Several months later, I was in my apartment in Bensonhurst when the phone rang around eleven o'clock at night. Mr. Victor was on the other end.

"Come over right now," he said. "Take a taxi."

I immediately sensed a strong hint of desperation in his voice. "What's wrong?"

"Never mind. Just come right away—and hurry!"

I quickly put on my fur coat over my nightgown. Wearing slippers, I took a taxi to the Regency Hotel in Manhattan where Mr. Victor maintained an apartment on the 14th floor. Like everything else in Mr. Potamkin's world, his apartment was a showplace. Two closets were filled with his suits, a chromed coffee table was topped with pictures of his grandchildren and two sons, king-sized bed with leopard skin spread, and walls covered with African art and Peter Max drawings. When I walked into Mr. Potamkin's bedroom, he was lying on the floor in dire pain, having awakened five hours earlier to discover he had shingles.

Peter Max drawing
(Victor and I).

Peter Max
drawing on
napkin.

Peter Max.

"What can I do for you, Mr. Victor?"

He asked me to put hot towels on his back, which I did until eight o'clock the next morning. Hot compresses were the only thing that gave him any relief, which he learned from several of his friends who had suffered with shingles. Seeing I was tired, Mr. Victor told me I could sleep in the guest bedroom.

"Sleep? I have to be at work in two hours, and here I am at eight in the morning wearing a nightgown, slippers, and a fur coat!"

"Oh. What now?" he said. "What're you going to do?"

"What am I going to do?" I replied, completely dumbfounded. "Sir, I—"

He broke out laughing.

"This is nothing to laugh about," I complained.

Mr. Potamkin called his secretary and instructed her to procure a new uniform for me in my size. An hour later, his secretary arrived with a uniform, and I barely made it to work. While I didn't know it at the time, my coming to Mr. Victor's aid when he was in need resulted in a far greater trust and responsibility in later years.

With Victor at a ski resort in Aspen, Colorado.

From that day, Mr. Potamkin requested that I come to his suite at five-thirty in the morning. I arrived every morning on time and applied compresses and prescription creams, then on my lunch break at work returned to his apartment and again cleaned his sores and applied hot compresses and topical medication.

After doing this for two months, Mr. Potamkin told me that I needed to move to Manhattan so that I didn't have to make the long trek from Brooklyn, and leased a comfortable two-bedroom apartment for me and Anna at East 82nd and 2nd Avenue. Now much closer to the Regency Hotel, I walked every morning two dozen blocks to Park Avenue. When Mr. Potamkin asked why I was walking, I told him the walk was good for me. He said it was better that I take a taxi, which I started doing.

One afternoon when I dropped by his office with his medications, he said, "How much money do you have in the bank, now that you're working two jobs?"

"Sir, I work one job."

"You're still working as a manicurist, right?"

"Yes."

"Then you have two jobs—one working at the salon and one working part time for me."

I paused in thought, hesitant, then finally said, "Mr. Potamkin, you don't pay me anything."

Mr. Victor looked surprised and was temporarily speechless, then said, "That's not correct. Nobody works for me for free." He leaned over and spoke into his intercom, "Mary, how much are we paying Jolanta?"

"Which Jolanta?" his secretary replied from her adjacent office.

"Our Jolanta!"

Five minutes later, Mr. Victor finally got off the phone with his accountant and told me that I would be paid 300 dollars a week. I thanked him. After I applied the next round of hot compresses and creams, he told me he was raising my pay to 600 dollars a week because he figured out that 300 was nothing. Again I thanked him.

"And don't ask me for a raise."

"Thank you."

Truth be known, I didn't care what Mr. Victor paid me, or even if he paid me at all. It was nice to do something for him because he was such an important person. Just being with him and working for him was a huge boost to my ego.

After Mr. Potamkin and I got to know each other, he commented that I was one of the best salespersons he ever knew and jokingly added that he feared that one day I might outsell him and he'd never know when. In time, he added me to his social list, and I began attending many of his lavish social functions, including his annual company party.

Mr. Potamkin had many admirable traits, one of which was that he preferred being informal. We often ate at the Palace restaurant because the restaurant served the best steak and the owner's son had married Mr. Victor's granddaughter Lisa. One time when we were having dinner out with company, I addressed him as Mr. Victor.

His cousin interrupted and said, "That's incorrect, Jolanta— either Victor or Mr. Potamkin, but not Mr. Victor."

In Poland, addressing someone by their first name preceded by "Mister" is a sign that they're important, so for me this was a habit. The same applies to women, for example Miss Leona for Leona Helmsley. In Poland many addressed me as Miss Jolanta.

Victor Potamkin was truly unpretentious. One never got the sense that he was extraordinarily rich. Sometimes when he was going out, he was concerned about overdressing. One night I commented, "Mr. Victor, you look like a millionaire." He gave me a displeased look, and I added, "I'm sorry, but you do."

He was a plain guy who never looked down on anyone. He much preferred the company of average, hardworking people, which is not unusual for the offspring of European immigrants. When Mr. Hess celebrated his birthday on March 14th, Mr. Potamkin chose to not attend because he felt uncomfortable around super wealthy people and knew there would be hundreds of them at Mr. Hess's party. So Mr. Potamkin bought an expensive watch and asked me to show it to Mr. Hess, and then give it to him only if he liked it. Mr. Potamkin wanted a connection with Mr. Hess, but only through me. As it turned out, Mr. Hess thought the watch was beautiful, and so I gave it to him, along with a birthday card from Mr. Potamkin.

One afternoon a woman reporter stopped by Mr. Victor's lavish Westside office to interview him for an article she was writing. I was present and watched him load her lap with a stuffed animal, an autographed copy of Liz Smith's latest book, a gift box of Norell cologne and a scarf, plus one of his business cards, which was a dollar bill with a picture of him pasted over George Washington. That afternoon I learned a major Potamkin precept—you never leave Mr. Victor's presence without a gift. He loved helping people and spreading his fortune around.

He was also the consummate entertainer who had practiced doing magic tricks since he was a kid. Often at social gatherings he would perform one of his favorite high rolling illusions on three different people. In each case he'd ask them for a dollar bill and then proceeded to fold it up in postage stamp size—this he abracadabra-ed into a 100 dollar bill for each of the wowed guests to keep. "After all, what is money but a magic trick?" Mr. Victor would blurt out with laughter, leaving the takers stunned.

Working conditions had not improved for me at Sal Fodera's salon. Although I did my best to steer clear of that older Spanish woman, Nuri, she tried everything to get me fired. One morning Mr. Fodera called us to his office and said, "Nuri, this is Jolanta's place. I don't care how many years you've worked with me. One day I'm going to take your stuff and put it in the garbage, and kick you out. Capisce?"

Nuri then took a different approach and began putting tiny pieces of cotton thread in my jars of nail polish, which could easily turn a 20 minute manicure into an hour manicure. She did many other things to sabotage my job. One Sunday morning when I opened the salon to give a private manicure, I discovered my uniform in the garbage with a banana peel stuffed in the front pocket. That was enough. On Monday morning, I went to Mr. Fodera and demanded an apology from Nuri, but when I was unable to prove that Nuri was responsible for any of my complaints, leaving Mr. Fodera's hands tied, I gave my notice and left the salon, which turned out to be a good decision because now I could work for Mr. Potamkin full time.

Mr. Victor had a girlfriend named Michelle when Luba was living, although Luba was in the final stages of Alzheimer's. Initially, Mr. Potamkin passed off Michelle as his "friend's daughter," the story being that a close friend of Mr. Victor had died and Mr. Potamkin had promised to take care of his friend's daughter.

I said, "Yeah, you're doing very well. You're overdoing it, Mr. Victor. Do you see a sign stupid on my forehead? Don't give me this baloney. It's your life; it's your business; I'm working for you, and with me everything is okay." Although I was surely overstepping my boundaries, I wanted Mr. Victor to know that he had one hundred percent of my loyalty and acceptance in all matters. Over time, I believe I am the only person that he honestly felt that he could trust unconditionally with everything.

When I worked for Mr. Potamkin, although he was the president of the largest car dealership in the entire world, he didn't give me a car because I had a chauffeured limousine at my disposal downstairs 24-hours. My driver was a Polish man named Robert who was jealous of my position with Mr. Potamkin and didn't like being my chauffeur. One day he made a point of not opening the door for me. Mr. Potamkin roared, "Robert, you open the door for Jolanta!" This one hundred percent loyalty that I extended to Mr. Potamkin was equally extended to me by him and was greatly appreciated. One day the irony occurred to me when I recalled that one evening after I had kicked Mr. Schreiber out of bed and we were having coffee in his kitchen, he had said to me that I shouldn't be a chauffeur but should have my own chauffeur.

Robert complied, and as I entered the back seating, I grinned and said, "Thank you, Robert."

LEFT: Victor
with funny-
man George
Burns.
BELOW:
Victor's
home in
Atlantic City,
New Jersey.

In the same manner that Mr. Hess enjoyed chasing and entertaining his own little obsessions (the Christmas goose), Mr. Victor now and then had his own extravagances. One day we were sitting in his living room at his apartment at the Regency Hotel and watching television when he casually mentioned that he was moving into the penthouse. A week later when everything was moved, he suddenly decided that he didn't like the penthouse. Although he pointed out that it offered a breathtaking view of the New York skyline, how often was it that anyone sitting outside looked at the New York skyline? So he decided to move again—this time to the apartment being vacated by one of the richest people in the world, Preston Robert Tisch, who owned the Regency Hotel and was in the process of building a luxurious penthouse apartment for himself and moving out of his apartment on the 14th floor.

Mr. "Bob" Tisch was an American businessman who was the chairman and part owner of the Loews Corporation and half-owner of the New York Giants football team. Along with his

Dinner party with Peter Max, Peter Max's father, Victor, me, Anna, Chauffeur.

brother, Bob Tisch added up to a quintessential Big Apple success story, beginning with playing stickball on the streets of Brooklyn to building to a financial conglomerate with annual sales of more than $15.2 billion and assets of $73.7 billion.

Mr. Tisch's enthusiasm for convening the city's movers and shakers began during the city's fiscal crisis in the 1970s with breakfasts at the Regency. Major players in that municipal drama—labor leader Victor Gotbaum, real estate mogul Lewis Rudin, and investment banker Felix G. Rohatyn—were the first regulars. "Stop over for breakfast, and you'll meet a lot of people," Mr. Tisch was famous for saying. Many credit him with coining the term "power breakfast," and the Regency continued to attract the likes of Beverly Sills, Henry Kissinger, and New York Mayor David Dinkins. Mr. Tisch's power breakfast was from the hotel's regular menu; the seating being sectioned off and was by invitation only. Victor Potamkin was among the list of regular attendees.

Mr. Potamkin said, "Go look at the Bob Tisch's apartment and tell me if you like it."

"Mr. Victor, I like what you like. It's not mine."

"Okay, I'll decide."

What was to decide? Mr. Tisch's 4,000 square foot apartment had too many bedrooms and bathrooms to count, the entire 14th floor, beautiful imported tile everywhere, art deco, and a movie theater for 50 people. One of Bob Tisch's many guests one night, after getting lost when searching for the guest bathroom, stated that the apartment should have its own zipcode!

Most evenings I'd sit with Mr. Potamkin and watch television while sipping grand livre. Initially, he coached me how to drink it because the first time I tried, I started choking. I was extremely grateful that he was willing to coach me about so many aspects of life about which I had little experience. The truth is that I learned more from Mr. Victor in a few years than I learned from my own father throughout my father's lifetime.

Unlike my father who never worked until he became an adult, Victor Potamkin started working at the age of five and from an early age had faced life on life's terms and did a remarkable job of it. One day he told me that we were so familiar in many ways, although I never understood what he meant by that. To me, he was this enormously powerful and accomplished man, and I was just Jolanta, a hardworking manicurist.

Of all the great lessons I learned from Mr. Victor it was that I shouldn't be so naïve. It was true that my naivety had caused me a great deal of hurt. Mr. Victor once said to me that people sometimes mistook my politeness for stupidity. He taught me to be confident, but by the same token portraying myself as a little pussy cat encouraged people to ask me what I wanted.

Although at first I was intimidated by Mr. Victor, with the passage of time I began to relax to the point that I could honestly enjoy him. When he was ill, I would sleep overnight in one of the guestrooms and get up throughout the night to check on his covers and make sure he was all right. Once he cut his toe on the leg of an armchair and was bleeding profusely because he was taking blood thinners. He didn't call an ambulance or his doctor; he just relied on me because he felt that I could take care of everything. So I decided to sleep in his bedroom next to his king-sized bed. When I thought he had fallen asleep, I snuck in and placed a pillow beside his bed and slept on the floor, so that every time he got up, I had control of what was happening.

Weeks later I was assured by one of his staff that he wasn't aware of my sleeping on the floor, until one evening when we went to dinner with his sons. I hadn't decided what to wear, so I told them to go downstairs and that I would join them, and that Mr. Victor knew what I liked to eat and could order for me.

When I arrived downstairs and walked into the dining room, Mr. Victor was seated at the head of the table, telling stories and waving his arms around flamboyantly like he was directing an orchestra. He suddenly pointed to me and announced to his sons, "Jolanta is sleeping on the floor already for a full month!"

Visibly embarrassed, all I could utter was, "Really?"

Mr. Victor and the others laughed. He had known for some

With Victor's two sons at his private jet.

time that I was sleeping on the floor but didn't say anything until this moment because he wanted me to think I was so clever sneaking into his room and hiding my pillow in his closet. I should have known better, given the fact that he had raised two boys.

October 26, 1993 was a long awaited day for me because it was the day I became a citizen of the United States. To be honest, although I was exhilarated beyond belief about finally becoming a citizen after all my years of study, the actual swearing in ceremony left much to be desired.

It seemed I had been getting dressed up for this day for months. When I arrived at the government building where the ceremony was to take place, I expected far more than a large room that resembled a courtroom that was jam-packed with approximately 1,000 people. I could hardly breathe when I heard my named called to recite the Pledge of Allegiance. There was no party afterwards. I just took the subway home, spent the night by myself, and went to work the next day.

My US Citizenship certificate.

The good news was that for me one of my main goals was finally accomplished. The United States was now my land, and I earned the right to be here. I was as much of an American as anyone else.

After I became an American citizen, I looked for Tony Avento, who had helped me obtain my green card, because now it was my turn to invite him and his wife (I was hoping they had married) to dinner. When I finally discovered his whereabouts, I called him on the phone. Upon hearing my voice and the news that I was now finally a citizen, said, "I still remember you."

"When can we have dinner?" I asked. "I haven't forgotten our agreement to toast champagne together when I became a citizen."

"You're not going to recognize me," he laughed. "Because I no longer have hair. Because of my hard work trying to get you your green card, I'm now bald."

"Yes, I saw your picture on my computer. Did you marry that beautiful lady?"

"Soon. We're engaged."

"Congratulations. I'm not surprised. I could tell how much she was in love with you. When you marry, I'm inviting you to Poland for your honeymoon."

We ended the conversation, leaving things hanging once

again with another invitation to be fulfilled sometime in the distant future. But he never called again to let me know he and his fiancé had gotten married.

In the winter of 1993, I learned that Richard Cantarella was sick when I received a letter from him telling me that he had lung cancer. He wrote that he was getting better and asked that I call him, which I did. We talked on the phone for three hours. I felt sorry that he was dying at such a young age and knew that the prognosis was grim. As I listened to his kind, soft voice over the phone, I realized that he had done nothing wrong except for not keeping his promise that we would move from Rahway. We just didn't understand each other. My English wasn't good, and he didn't know me mentally. When we were married, Richard didn't understand how important my surroundings are to me.

After we divorced, I never understood why he didn't retire and enjoy life, and I told him he should take time off and travel. For once he took my advice and traveled to London. When he returned, he called to thank me, telling me that he now enjoyed traveling to Europe and would be doing a lot more travel. But now it was too late. At the end of our conversation, he asked if I had a boyfriend or if I was married.

"No!" I replied. "Nobody deserves me!"

He laughed, and then asked if I would marry him again, only this time under my conditions. I didn't want to get married, but I also didn't want to upset him because he was so sick, so I told him I would think about it.

Two days later, Richard Cantarella passed away in his sleep.

For a long time, I was saving money so that I could to invite my parents to the United States to visit. Finally when I had enough money saved, I bought airline tickets. Also, because we would need more space, Anna and I moved to a beautiful penthouse apartment on Roosevelt Island that was paid for by Mr. Potamkin's company as part of my salary. The building had a beautiful green marble lobby where the management served a continental breakfast every morning, a 24-hour doorman and

ABOVE: My mother visiting me. By now she needed a cane to get around
New York. BELOW: At Victor's apartment with my parents, Anna and her
boyfriend and Victor.

concierge, pool, and state-of-the-art fitness center. Best of all, the apartment had a sweeping view of Manhattan and was two minutes from the Regency Hotel—one stop by subway underwater. In expectation of my mother's arrival, I decorated the guest bedroom where my mother would be staying with beautiful art, house plants, and perfumed candles.

I was overwhelmed with joy when my parents—especially my mother—finally arrived from Poland. Because Mr. Potamkin knew how much my mother meant to me, he invited us all to dinner at his penthouse apartment at the Regency Hotel. While my mother was in New York, he treated her like a queen, and even gave me the full use of his limousine to take her around the Big Apple, as well as paid for a fabulous night on the town that included VIP treatment at New York's top Broadway play.

For three years I was employed as Mr. Potamkin's companion and caregiver. My responsibilities included running the affairs of his many residences, maintaining Mr. Victor's busy social and travel schedule, as well as supervising his medications and doctor appointments.

If I approved something, it was like Mr. Potamkin approved it. Even when I accompanied him to the hospital, if I stepped out of Mr. Potamkin's room, the doctor was instructed to wait until I returned because I was Mr. Victor's spokesperson.

In the final year of his life, Mr. Potamkin was hospitalized twice—the first time in New York, and his last hospital admission in Miami. Manhattan is a difficult place to be for a sick person. When his heart began to fail him near the end, he asked me which hospital he should be admitted to. I told him Miami because he had donated a substantial amount of money to help build that hospital and I personally knew the hospital's chief cardiologist.

I sat at his bedside for the entire two weeks of his hospitalization. The most difficult thing I have ever had to do in my entire life was when I had to authorize on June 7, 1995 that Mr. Potamkin's life support be disconnected. I cried for an entire week and could barely get through his funeral. As a footnote, Mr. Victor's wife Luba died a year and two months earlier of complications from Alzheimer's disease.

Prior to the final year of Victor Potamkin's life, I thought of him as an invaluable mentor. Today he would be in high demand as what is commonly referred to as a life coach. But he was much more than that. On a personal level, he was the first man who ever supported me emotionally. When I went to bed at night, I felt greatly relieved that there was a man in this world whom I trusted and sincerely cared about me and had my best interest at heart. Before Mr. Victor came into my life, I'd never had a man who watched over me. More than anything else that Mr. Victor gave me, that he gave me his 100 percent friendship was the most treasured gift of all.

Health care proxy for Victor.

CHAPTER ELEVEN

THE RETURN OF THE ENTREPRENEUR

I was grateful to Mr. Potamkin for leaving me money in his will. Before he died, he told me to go back to Poland because, in his opinion, I was too good for the United States. Initially, I thought he was joking, but later wondered if there wasn't a bit of truth to his words because now and then he would ask me if I had thought about returning to Poland to restore my farm—if I had the money, that is? "After all," he once commented, "if you did well in Poland once with a small government loan, imagine what you could do with a full pocket of private money."

Five months after Victor died, Anna felt that she was old enough to live on her own and wanted her independence. In record time, once she had made this decision, she had a job and began attending school.

When she left, I starting thinking what to do with my expensive 2,000 square foot penthouse apartment in Roosevelt Island? If nothing else, I was beginning to feel a bit selfish about enjoying all the extravagance, so I invited my friend Halina and my jeweler from Bialystok, who brought a gentleman named Mark Goworek. After discussing a shared tenancy, the four of us agreed to divide the apartment in half—the two men would live in one half, and the two women would live in the other half.

My three roommates were supposed to move to the apartment in three weeks. Then five days before they were to move in, Mark came to the apartment and said that he had an idea, which was that he and I would split the apartment between the two of us because he felt that the apartment would be too crowded with four people.

After giving his idea thought, I said, "Okay, if you want to pay twice as much rent." The money didn't matter to me. I just hated wasting this beautiful apartment and, besides, I've always been a family oriented person who much prefers living with others than living by myself.

Mark moved in and everything went smoothly. A platonic relationship worked quite naturally for me because I really had no time to devote to a relationship.

A month into our roommate arrangement, he wanted to invite his wife to come over from Poland but said that she could be uncomfortable with my being here. "No problem," I said. "I'll take a vacation. Invite her. We're roommates, so we have to make compromises."

Regardless of my offer to leave the apartment while Mark's wife visited, she simply didn't like the idea of her husband living with another woman and told Mark she wasn't coming. This was really unnecessary. Mark was a fair husband. He didn't have a girlfriend and talked constantly about his family. Like me, he was focused mainly on his work and sending money back to Poland.

One invitation to Mark's wife expired, then another. Finally, he told his wife that he was sending one more invitation, and that if she didn't come to see him, then he was going to divorce her. When she turned down his third invitation, he went through with the divorce.

I had for some time wanted to create a school environment where children could be taught social graces, elegance in manners and poise, and appreciation for the fine arts. In order to prepare for this, I completed an extensive training course at the Protocol School of Washington (DC), which is a school of etiquette, from which I received my accreditation. At that time, this was the only etiquette school in the United States, with its classes being held at the Ritz Hotel. Because I couldn't teach etiquette without certification, I went to Washington DC to become certified.

The word "etiquette" has an interesting origin. When Louis XIV's palace gardener at Versailles discovered that aristocrats were trampling through his gardens, he put up signs, or *etiquets*, to warn them off—thus creating the first "keep off the grass" sign. When the dukes and duchesses walked right past the signs, anyway, the king himself had to decree that no one was to go beyond the grounds of *etiquets*. Later, the meaning of etiquette was expanded to include the ticket to court functions that listed the rules on where to stand and what to do.

I was motivated to attend etiquette school because I felt there was an absence of etiquette in the United States. Many of the children I met in New York were loud and impolite. I wanted to make a difference by teaching etiquette because America was my new country, my new home, and my daughter was going to grow up here. More importantly, because of the difficult experiences that I faced when I first came to the United States, I wanted to help newly-arrived emigrants.

With Mrs. Johnson at Etiquette school in Washington DC.

Etiquette in Europe has always been more important than in America, perhaps if for no other reason than Europe is a much older society. What I learned from my classes at the Protocol School in Washington, DC was that in America until the 1960s good manners were considered part of a child's upbringing. Public and private schools included etiquette as part of a well-rounded curriculum, and charm schools specialized in the social graces.

Because of the Vietnam War, social unrest, and the influx of drugs (the Hippie Revolution), the '60s and '70s brought about a decline in the popularity of etiquette programs, whereas in the '90s, with the arrival of the Yuppie Generation, the strong emphasis on family values and education and a demand for etiquette programs nationwide was unprecedented and far exceeded the supply. Unquestionably, the return of traditional values in the '90s was bringing about an increased appreciation of good manners.

I opened my private etiquette school (*Design for Life*) in New York on 7th Avenue and 39th Street and signed a two-year lease on a commercial office space that was in shambles and was slated to be torn down. I had $100,000 to invest, and Mark Goworek, who was a hardworking person and soon became my best friend, helped me fix up the place. I moved into the top floor, which I completely renovated—installing new parquet flooring, and painting and wallpapering the walls. The lobby was deplorable, so Mark and I stripped the floor, painted the staircase, and put flowers everywhere.

Monday when the cleaning person arrived, I watched him on the security camera, and he looked confused, as if he had entered the wrong building. He called the landlord, who came over and, on seeing my miraculous renovations, said, "Jolanta, we have to talk. You're paying $200 a month less rent."

That was fine with me. And there was more. "Do me a favor," I replied. "We don't need this cleaning person. We can do the cleaning."

"Great! Then take off another hundred!"

We had a fantastic arrangement, and my landlord ended up

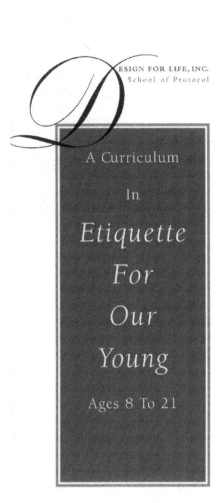

ESIGN FOR LIFE, INC.
School of Protocol

A Curriculum

In

Etiquette
For
Our
Young

Ages 8 To 21

RIGHT: Etiquette
school brochure.
BELOW: Remodeling
etiquette school,
social club with Mark.

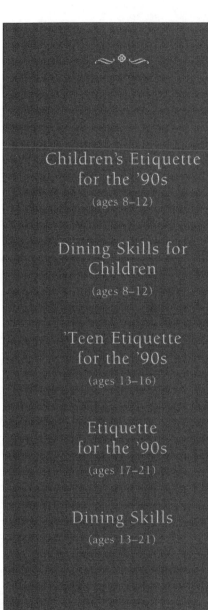

Children's Etiquette for the '90s
(ages 8–12)

Dining Skills for Children
(ages 8–12)

'Teen Etiquette for the '90s
(ages 13–16)

Etiquette for the '90s
(ages 17–21)

Dining Skills
(ages 13–21)

*W*hen Jolanta Soysal arrived in New York from Poland in 1987, she began the task of realizing her dream of creating a school where children would be taught the important social graces, elegance in manners and poise, and appreciation of fine quality in their surroundings.

Ms. Soysal spent eight years in preparing herself for the realization of her vision. She worked as a consultant for a number of years in high end salons, among them Elizabeth Arden, salons at the St. Regis Hotel, the Pierre Hotel, the Waldorf Astoria and the Harmonie Club. There she was fortunate to make the acquintance of well-known people, among them President Reagan, Princess Di, King Hussein of Jordan and his family, artist Peter Max, opera star Rise Stevens, Leona Helmsley, and photographer Franchesco Scavullo. She earned a Certificate in Interior Design from The Shefield School of Interior Design and she completed an extensive training course at The Protocol School of Washington® (DC) from where she received her accreditation.

Ms. Soysal is delighted to be opening her school, located just two blocks north of New York's famous Fashion Institute of Technology. She has assembled a qualified staff of consultants that specialize in various aspects of manners and etiquette. She invites you to call her for more details and a for a schedule of times when classes are offered.

ESIGN FOR LIFE, INC.
School of Protocol

(212)947-1313

360 Seventh Avenue, New York,NY 10018 (212)947-1666 Fax

Etiquette school brochure.

renting the entire building because when prospective tenants would come, the landlord would show them the top floor that Mark and I had renovated. Our floor became the model floor for the building—and the prospective tenants ended up signing a lease. Over the long run, I saved the landlord's building that was destined a year earlier for demolition.

My *Design for Life*'s School of Protocol program offered an up-to-date etiquette curriculum for children, teens, and young adults that built confidence and self-esteem by teaching social and communication skills.

Etiquette is simple, but people have to be taught how to be polite. For example, I often watch the television news and see anchorwomen half-naked in front of the camera. This is not etiquette. These women need sleeves. It's not pleasurable to see a half-naked anchorwoman, even when she is beautiful, reporting that hundreds of people have died in a plane crash.

Life is a theater, and often the role a person plays is defined by the costume they display. A person who puts on a white coat is a doctor. A man who puts on a white collar and black coat is a priest. I put on a manicurist uniform and I'm a manicurist. Depending on the costume a person puts on, they can be whatever they want to be.

Etiquette is a foundation of life. When a person knows etiquette—better still, if they are taught etiquette from early childhood—they live a respectable life with ambition. Etiquette teaches a person something as simple as shaking hands. Manners is only a small part of a big map. Some people used to ask me to give them a tip about etiquette. A person can't learn etiquette from a few tips. Etiquette must be embraced by one's being to the degree that it becomes natural.

I taught my daughters etiquette at an early age. When Anna attended her first day of kindergarten, she asked the teacher, "Where is my silverware?"

The teacher replied, "Anna, you have a spoon."

"I see a spoon, but a spoon is for soup. For meat I need a fork and knife." Anna was the only child in the class who asked about silverware.

In 1996, etiquette wasn't popular. I advertised on a public bulletin board at the Polish embassy and got a few students. Ultimately, teaching etiquette in New York turned out not to be as popular as I first thought. Because everything was too expensive, my ad netted only a few students. Generally speaking, New Yorkers weren't the tea and crumpet crowd that Londoners are.

When the etiquette school failed, I got to thinking about what Victor Potamkin had suggested to me several years earlier—that I consider going back into business in Poland. This was a good time for me to consider this because Poland was finally on the rebound, and everyone was breathing a sigh of relief.

In the early 1990s in Poland, a shock therapy program enabled the country to transform its socialist-style planned economy into a market economy, and by 1995 Poland was thriving. Most visibly, there were numerous improvements in human rights that included freedom of speech and an open access to an uncensored Internet.

In early 1997, I traveled to Poland and asked the government officials the right way to go about opening a new business. I wanted to become the Leona Helmsley of Poland and open a 40-room hotel in Bialystok. I had the land where my chicken farm used to be and also had acquired 40 rooms of luxurious used hotel furniture (including decorations and vacuums) from Mr. Tisch. In addition, I purchased two vehicles—a passenger van for the hotel and a Cadillac DeVille for my daughter Jolanta—from Mr. Potamkin's car dealership in Miami.

One week later, I had everything shipped to Poland and shortly thereafter arrived back in Bialystok to meet with the architects who were going to design my hotel. Almost immediately, I was made aware of a slight "snag"—the government informed

After chicken farm closed down and I sold the land.

me that I needed to pay taxes on the furnishings and motor vehicles that I had brought into Poland. To my utter horror, the government wasn't asking for a nominal import tax. They were demanding that I pay a 100 percent tax on everything!

At first I thought this was a clerical error or some misunderstanding, but soon realized it wasn't. I had battled the government before and was willing to battle them again. I had the furniture in storage and the two motor vehicles parked in my son-in-law's garage, although the government would not permit the vehicles to be driven and even kept the keys.

I then hired an attorney and sued the government, and after two years won my case. I never saw coming what came next, and neither did my attorney—although I was no longer required to pay this 100 percent tax, the government now claimed that I owed them $400,000 for two years of storage fees!

That was the final straw. I was done. Poland could have all my furniture, which I told them on no uncertain terms that I hoped they would not enjoy. My two vehicles, however, were another matter. After being put in touch with a customs officer who worked the border between Poland and Russia, I arranged for both vehicles to be slipped across the border late one night, and then the next morning reported to the authori-

With my sister Alicja around 1989.

ties in Bialystok that both vehicles had disappeared. Ultimately, both vehicles were sold to the Russian mafia, which allowed me to recoup a substantial amount of the money I had paid for them.

Thus ended my business in Poland, and I left with no intention of ever doing business in my homeland country again. Although communism had supposedly ended back in 1989, Poland had the same system of government, only it was now called a democracy.

Upon returning to the United States, I again focused on my commercial lease and ultimately decided to convert the failed School of Protocol program from its parent *Design for Life* program and open a social club for emigrates arriving in New York.

Design for Life had a good meaning—a design for work or for whatever the person wanted to do. My excitement about life was renewed because I was helping others by teaching my knowledge to newly-arrived emigrants. I especially wanted to impress upon

Before and after of the remodeling of the social club.

ESIGN FOR LIFE, INC.
United Immigrants

You're not alone
Fulfilling immigrants dreams, step by step

For the last two hundred years history repeats itself. Immigrants, young and old, are coming to America to start a new life and fulfill dreams about freedom and self-realization. They are coming to the United States to become citizens of the country which offers unlimited potential for creative and dynamic individuals.
Those who are strongest and most entrepreneurial can make it to the top.
But unfortunately, hundreds of thousands of new immigrants never get a chance to become useful and productive citizens. Instead of helping America stay the strongest, most dynamic and innovative economy they end up in ghettos, doing menial job and never utilizing their full potential.
Immigrants are innovators, entrepreneurs, doctors, artists, teachers, and businessmen. Very often they belong to the most dynamic and best-educated parts of society in their home country. Quite often they waste enormous amount of time and energy dealing with trivial and simple everyday problems which, for them, can become insurmountable obstacles.
Design for Life, Inc. was created to help immigrants to quickly adapt and contribute to the new society. We realize that with a little help, some information and proper direction coupled with encouragement immigrants can very quickly become leaders and innovators. Once they combine their education with language abilities and knowledge of their new country immigrants quickly become productive citizens and leaders of their new communities.
Design for Life, Inc. is doing everything possible to shorten transitory period in which immigrants adjust to the new society. For the last two years we created an extended family of 4,000 people who participated in our courses, trip classes, concerts, social events and exhibitions. Some of them are Americans that are willing to help; some are immigrants that need all the help they can get.
Thanks to our programs recent immigrants could learn both English and French, get acquainted with history of United States and learn about different parts of the world. They could relax and share a laugh during dance classes, violin concerts and cabaret presentations.
Our programs offered excellent networking possibilities. Lectures about everyday problems showed simple solutions to problems immigrants thought to be very difficult. Graduates of our English classes went on with their education—some started to attend colleges and universities, others got promoted or changed jobs, for ones that would better utilize their skills.
Every day we receive telephone calls thanking for support and advice. We are happy that with so little we were able to put smiles on so many faces.
We will continue to fulfill dreams of immigrants. We will help them find in America a place they can call home.

510 Main Street, Room 1324 New York, NY 10044 Tel.: 212 753-7902

Design for Life welcoming letter.

them the importance of learning English and that speaking good English is the foundation to everything.

Unlike most of the romance languages of Europe, English is an unfriendly language because it has so many slang words and expressions. When someone first comes to the United States, it's difficult to learn all the inside lingo—for example in the '90s "Chill out" meant calm down, "My bad" meant my mistake, "Freak out" meant to go crazy, "Don't go there" implied a touchy subject, and "Cha-ching" meant that something was costly.

Moreover, 25 years ago a Polish person who needed to find a restroom in Manhattan had a major problem, especially if they didn't speak English. Today men and women's restrooms are clearly indicated by images of a man and a woman that are posted over the entrances to both restrooms. But decades ago, all that was indicated were signs that read "Men" and "Women."

Or what if a European emigrant encountered an emergency and needed to go to a hospital? How could they ask for help or directions, let alone read signs, if they didn't know English?

I've always had a strong need to be surrounded by family, which, sorrowfully was lacking whenever I was in the United States and away from Poland. Most Americans don't have a strong family connection like that of the Italians, Greeks, and Jews, for example.

Family is my foundation because I know my parents loved and needed me, and they took good care of me and worried about me constantly. They devoted a tremendous amount of time raising me properly and made considerable sacrifices. Without family, I'd be on the street somewhere in a week. My family helped shape my life, especially my mother. She gave me a solid work ethic and taught me to love family and life. By the time I left home and became a wife and mother, I had all I needed to begin life as an adult.

When I left Poland, however, I also left the majority of my family. The social club filled this void. Sometimes there would be 100 guests at the club, and I cooked for all of them, just as my

Enjoying social club. I'm definitely in my element.

LEFT: Social club member cutting birthday cake. ABOVE: Wedding at social club. BELOW: Party at social club.

mother had in Poland when I was a child. Some members and their friends came just to eat because they missed a good home cooked meal. The social club was a heartwarming family environment in which I gladly was everyone's mother, sister, confidant, and mentor.

When I opened the social club, it soon became so popular that I was doing television spots and writing articles in the Polish newspapers. The nationalities of the members was mixed, although there were no Russians. When I walked down the street—especially in Greenpoint—people knew me from the media coverage and thanked me for opening the club.

In addition to many social functions that were held at the club, such as dances, birthday, and even weddings, members enjoyed parties at the Polish Consulate, evening dinners that were held on boats, and even music recitals. For these outings, members paid 50 percent of the price. At the club there were English lessons, as well as French lessons; and we celebrated Easter and Christmas.

Polish newspaper party in New York that I helped organize.

NEW
VOICES

Weill Recital / Little Carnegie Hall
New York
Sunday, October 19th, 1997
8:30 p.m.

"Design for Life"
sponsored concert at
Carnegie Hall.

RIGHT: WITH Francesco Scavullo. BELOW: How to set a proper dinner table setting.

With actor Al Lewis, Grandpa on the *The Munsters.*

One of the many rewarding functions of the social club was helping emigrates find work, both part time and permanent. For example, one day I learned that one of our members, who was a licensed physician in Poland and had received his license to practice medicine in New York, was having no success in finding a job. When I learned of this, I told this person to give me a few days. After making a dozen phone calls, I was able to help obtain an interview for this person at a local hospital for a position as an assistant surgeon.

After I got the details, I called this young Polish doctor, who came right over and listened to what I had learned from a representative at the hospital's personnel office.

"Are you sure?" the doctor asked, then seemed to hold his breath.

"Well, no," I said in fairness. "Between us, I'm not sure because this would be a miracle."

"I'm going there now," the young man replied anxiously and

then hurriedly departed. Two hours later, he returned to the social club with flowers.

"I don't know how to say thank you. I got the job! I start on Monday!"

I was delighted. I knew that this doctor was highly gifted and well trained and would be a great addition to the hospital's medical staff.

Over the course of a year and a half, I mentored more than 4,000 people, the majority of them women. I freely taught ten women how to do manicures and facials. Well, not really for free because when they finished learning, I said, "All of you must pay back by teaching another ten women. And then you must instruct these ten women to teach another ten. It's going to be a great thing. And I'm going to find jobs for all of you—I promise—if you keep your promise to me."

I eventually found jobs in Manhattan for all of them. Around Christmas, a group of these women arrived unexpectedly at my workplace (I had since returned to working part-time as a cosmetologist). I heard the receptionist call my name and ask me to come to the front desk. When I arrived, I saw the women standing at the desk, smiling.

"What happened?"

One of them presented me with a small, nicely wrapped gift box and said, "It's Christmas time." When I opened the gift, I discovered a beautiful gold bracelet with each of their first names engraved on the back. These were just two of hundreds of similar gratifying moments.

Design for Life had been set up as a nonprofit corporation, with memberships costing $100 each. As to the daily operation, I have always been a one person orchestra, and the running of the social club was no exception. For the most part, I did all the cleaning, cooking, and teaching, as well as planning the events both at the club and outside the club.

Because of the wide media coverage, I one day received a call from a representative of MetLife who informed me that

Opening of social club at Regency Hotel with Anna
(Mr. Tisch paid for this).

Ryszard Kaczorowski, the last President of Poland in exile.

MetLife wanted to sponsor *Design for Life* and was offering to invest $160,000 to help with expansion. Although making money was not my primary reason for opening the social club, I was impressed and grateful that a company as powerful and far-reaching as MetLife recognized *Design for Life* 's potential.

My putting together the *Design for Life* social club ultimately turned out to be an example of the old adage "No good deed goes unpunished." As time progressed and the club became popular, a group of people started asking how much money I was making, which deeply hurt me. The truth was I was breaking even, if not losing money, because whatever profits were reinvested in the club.

These doubters asked for a meeting, to which I agreed. At the meeting, they asked how much money I spent on carpeting, how much for liquor, how much for this and for that. These people simply could not conceive of the idea that I didn't open the club to get rich. For the past year and a half, the club meant something to me that was far more valuable than money—it gave me the satisfaction that came from helping more than 4,000 emigrants become better equipped in their new lives.

The bad energy that was generated from people asking about money was more than hurtful—it was insulting. Finally, after two days of their constant belittling and nitpicking, I decided to close the club. I just couldn't live with the thought that people wrongly thought that I had opened the club for financial gain.

There would be more sadness. A short while after my mother returned to Poland, her arthritic knee was worsening, so much so that she decided to go ahead with a knee replacement. Although I had initially wanted her to have the surgery done in the United States (Mr. Hess had made all the arrangements), my mother didn't want to be a burden to me, and so she scheduled the operation to be done in Warsaw.

My daughter Jolanta was to keep me informed as to my mother's progress. All of the pre-op work went well, and a two days later my mother underwent what was a relatively simple knee replace-

Jolanta's wedding.

ment procedure. I waited by the phone to hear from Jolanta, and at some point became aware that the passing time and figured that the procedure either started late or was taking a bit longer.

Then the phone finally rang. Jolanta was on the other end. I could instantly tell by her voice that something was terribly wrong. Within moments, I learned that my mother was deceased, having died on the table during the operation. Apparently she had developed a blood clot in her leg that traveled to her lung and caused a fatal embolism.

Once again, a loved one had died who wasn't supposed to. My mother's operation was a simple one, and had it been done in the United States, I have no doubt that she would not have died. I felt the same way about my husband Andrew. Had those routine pre-op tests been done in Stockholm instead of Bialystok, Andrew also would not have died. I felt the same way about the death of my infant son that should have never happened. I guess that sometimes life is just this way—heartbreaking tragedies happen without reason.

I immediately traveled to Poland for my mother's funeral,

which was more devastating to me emotionally than when I had to authorize Victor Potamkin's discontinuation of his life support, which was followed by his funeral.

My daughters Anna and Jolanta were as distressed as I was. They truly loved their grandmother who had done as much for them as she had done for me.

The day my mother died, my life lost a tremendous pillar stone. I had zero problems when my mother was alive. Whenever I was faced with adversity, I called my mother, and after five minutes of talking with her, I was like a newborn baby without a care in the world. My mother made everything right and was my stabilizing rudder. Now that she was gone, I suddenly felt totally lost and no longer emotionally secure.

A short while after I returned to New York, Sister Regina Palamara, who was aware of my deep sorrow and despondency, invited me to come to her Parish where she ran a large thrift shop. She had recently lost her twin sister and felt that we would be good company for each other. Over the next several weeks, I

Sister Regina Palamara.

Gold bowls with my name inscribed on the bottoms.

worked at the thrift shop and completely reorganized the merchandise, painted the floor blue, and redecorated the entire store. My work there was so relaxing that I began to regularly volunteer, and at some point once again began to seriously consider becoming a nun. My dream was short lived, however, when Sister Regina convinced me that becoming a nun wasn't for me. So for the second time my dream of becoming a nun was dashed, although I did continue to volunteer at the thrift shop, which turned out to be a blessing. Months later, in recognition of my volunteer service, Sister Regina gifted me with two beautiful gold bowls.

After closing the social club, I began studying to become a real estate salesperson. My close friend owned a real estate company in Queens and was waiting for me to become licensed. Once licensed, I worked at the office in Queens, and then moved to a prestigious firm in Manhattan. Years earlier, Victor Potamkin had told me that I was a natural salesman, and now here was my chance to prove him right.

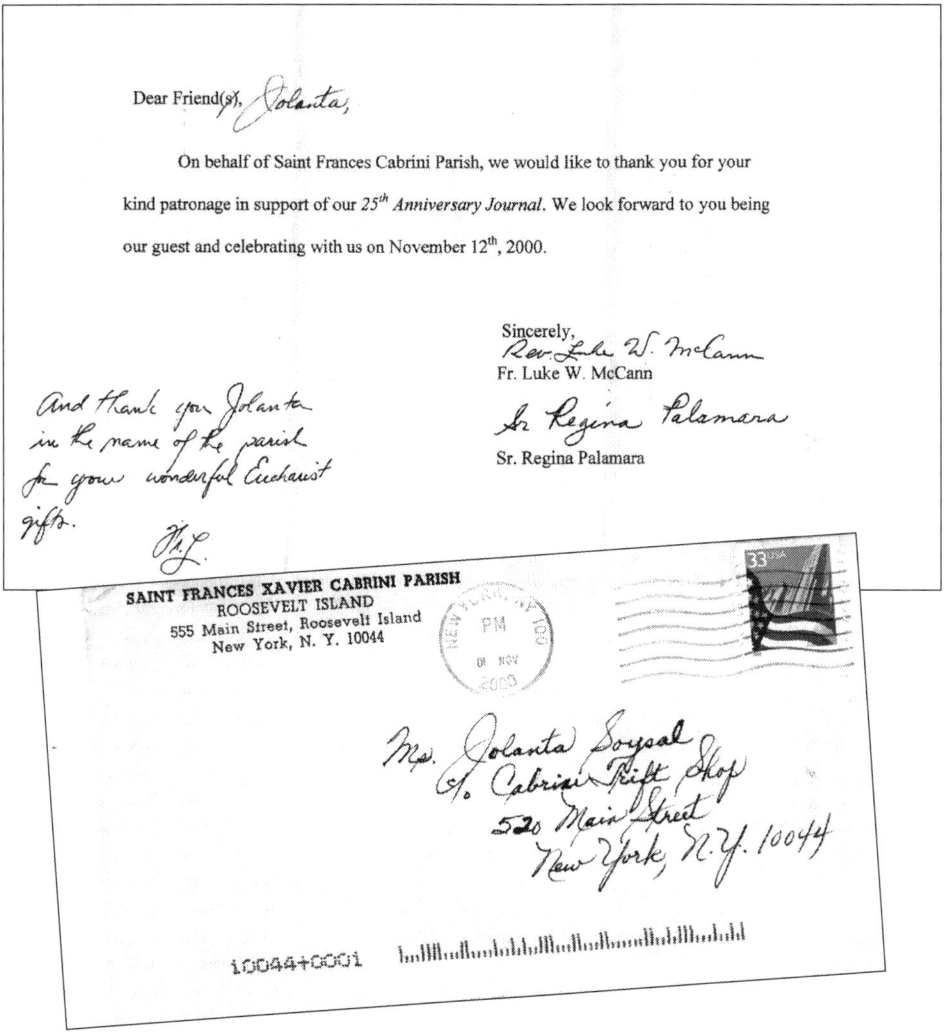

Dear Friend(s), *Jolanta,*

On behalf of Saint Frances Cabrini Parish, we would like to thank you for your

kind patronage in support of our 25*th* *Anniversary Journal*. We look forward to you being

our guest and celebrating with us on November 12*th*, 2000.

Sincerely,

Rev. Luke W. McCann
Fr. Luke W. McCann

Sr. Regina Palamara

Sr. Regina Palamara

And thank you Jolanta in the name of the parish for your wonderful Eucharist gifts.

H.L.

SAINT FRANCES XAVIER CABRINI PARISH
ROOSEVELT ISLAND
555 Main Street, Roosevelt Island
New York, N. Y. 10044

NEW YORK, NY
PM
01 NOV
2000

33 USA

Ms. Jolanta Soysal
C/o Cabrini Gift Shop
520 Main Street
New York, N.Y. 10044

10044+0001

Thank you note for my volunteer work.

After working hard for six months, I finally had a solid list of clients and was on the verge of closing escrow on a two million dollar apartment that was adjacent to the United Nations Building. Because I was representing both the seller and buyer, my commission was going to be substantial. Then three days before escrow was set to close, the bottom fell out from not only my escrow—but from the entire city of New York—when two skyjacked commercial jet airplanes slammed into the Twin Towers of the World Trade Center and brought America to its knees.

Terrified by what I was hearing, as well as seeing on the television news, I knew that I had to get out of my office that was located on the 55th floor of 55 Madisen Avenue. As I frantically made my way out of the building, I walked out into the streets to a sight that I shall never forget. Everywhere amid the billowing dust and smoke from the collapsed skyscrapers of the World Trade Center, thousands of people were running away from the escalating chaos. Many were injured and bleeding. The air was filled with screaming and the deafening wail of hundreds of sirens.

I lost my career in real estate that day because no one was going to buy anything in New York for a long time. Only a small percentage of the pending escrows in and around Manhattan closed, excluding mine. Property values were tenuous, to say the least. Among the thousands of others who lost their jobs, Mark was let go from his job working for an exclusive New York jeweler Christopher Designs at 5th Avenue and 48th Street.

In the ensuing weeks, with the exception of the cleanup crews, New York was a ghost town. One morning an old woman who was born and raised in New York silently handed me a tiny American flag that was affixed to a small wooden stick. She spoke no words, just a brief smile and a slight nod of her head. I had waited for so long to become a proud American, and now here I was holding the American flag given to me by a broken woman who still held out hope that America was going to do what she had done for over two centuries—survive.

CHAPTER TWELVE

GOOD BYE, NEW YORK

A fter the crisis of 9/11, I moved with Mark to Stroudsburg, Pennsylvania where he had purchased a parcel of land and was building a house. Stroudsburg is a borough in Monroe County and is approximately five miles from the Delaware Water Gap. Downtown Stroudsburg has 24 restaurants, 9 art galleries, 3 women's clothing stores, numerous antique stores, several general merchandisers, many specialty shops, 2 hotels, the local YMCA, 11 financial institutions and the core of the legal profession in Monroe County.

Living in Stroudsburg wasn't my choice. This New York bedroom community was far too traditional for my liking—surely a far cry from Manhattan—and the local people were close knit and didn't readily accept outsiders. The transition was emotionally distressing. At times I felt like I had gone from the penthouse to the outhouse, to quote an old saying. Over the years, however, I had become flexible, which was the result of one of my mother's favorite mottos: "If you can't have what you like, then like what you have."

My plan was to eventually move back to New York after the cleanup crews and building contractors restored the city to even a remote resemblance to what it was before 9/11. Meanwhile, I commuted to New Jersey by train.

While Mark busied himself during the day putting the finishing touches on the house, I went to work at Martin's Furniture Store in New Jersey. Martin's Furniture Store featured the high-end Bassett line of furniture that to this day is one of the more recognizable brands in America. Originally made of Appalachian

With Mark.

oak, Bassett furniture dates back to the late 1800s to the foothills of the Blue Ridge Mountains where the Bassett family operated a sawmill. The store manager hired me because a year earlier I had graduated from the Sheffield School of Interior Design (today the New York Institute of Art and Design).

One afternoon I was helping a lady who said, "What are you doing here? You don't belong here?"

Her comment caused me to laugh inside. This wasn't the first time I was told that I was in the wrong place. When I first arrived in New York, Charles Schreiber told me that I shouldn't be driving a limo, but should have my own limousine and driver. How ironic that it turned out he was right when a few years later Victor Potamkin provided me with my own limo and chauffeur. A few years later, Leona Helmsley told me that I should be in real estate. Again, how ironic that years later I ended up selling real estate in New York. Amused, I offered the woman a smile.

"Really? Where do I belong?"

"You belong in a jewelry store," she replied.

The truth was I had grown tired of selling furniture and welcomed the possibility of a change. The woman gave me her card and arranged for me to be interviewed for a sales position at Littman Jewelers, which is a major chain that has been in business for more than 100 years and is a subsidiary of Fred Meyers Jewelry.

On the day I arrived for my interview, I saw that the store had an attractive layout that featured handsome furniture, plush carpeting, and meticulously lit display cases. Not long into my conversation with the manager, she asked me what I knew about jewelry.

"Nothing," I replied honestly.

She considered me for several long moment, and then asked, almost quizzically, "So how do you plan to sell jewelry?"

I had anticipated her question.

"I'll learn. Give me three months. If I turn out to be a lousy salesperson, kick me out and the champagne is on me."

"Oh, my God," she sighed with a laugh.

"You have an open sales position that you need to fill, correct?"

"Yes."

"So this is my place, this is my job."

I could tell by her demeanor that, although she liked my straightforward approach, she didn't like me enough to hire a total novice.

"You'll have to talk to the store owner," she finally said cordially.

The next day I met with the owner. Within a few minutes our discussion reached the point it had reached with the store manager. "You're not losing anything," I said. "I'm losing three months. Give me three months, and I'll prove myself. I'm not a dummy."

I was hopeful that after all was said and done, the store's owner would realize that, because I would be working on a commission only basis, I was essentially a free employee. Why not roll the dice? After giving the matter some thought, he said, "I like you. Okay. When do you want to start?"

"Two days ago."

I was nervous on my first day, but I managed to relax and focus on the customers. I had learned a great deal from Victor Potamkin, who was the greatest car salesman in the history of the automobile industry. The key was to keep my attention focused on my customer. "Is the ring too small?" "Too big?" "Sit down and let me fix this problem." "Would you care for tea, coffee?"

If the customer selected a piece of jewelry that needed adjusting or enhancement, I'd race downstairs where there was a jeweler and give him the information. He'd fix the problem, clean and polish the piece, and I'd race back upstairs and close the sale.

Learning about jewelry wasn't difficult because every piece of jewelry had a tag that contained all the information. All I did was learn what each piece of information meant. Moreover, whenever another salesperson was making a sale, I'd eavesdrop. In my free time, I read books and perused Internet sites about jewelry and the art of salesmanship.

Besides mentors like Victor Potamkin, Leon Hess, and Bob Tisch, I learned a great deal from Leona Helmsley and soon became an excellent "instant read" of my customers. When a woman would enter the store, I'd schmooze with her for a couple of minutes and then ask her to show me her favorite piece of jewelry, upon which she'd lead me to where I needed to be to close a sale.

Most customers already know what they want long before they come to buy. All that's missing is a salesperson that bonds with that customer and essentially gives them permission to purchase what they already want. After three months, I sold the most expensive ring in the store—a $40,000 six caret marquise diamond of near perfect color and clarity.

I worked at that store for a year and eventually grew to hate the commute. Because of the store's location, it took several hours to travel between my work and home. At night, the drive was dangerous because there were deer on the road, which, because I've always been a devout animal lover who would wreck my car before hitting an animal (especially Bambi!), there were places along the road where I'd drive at a snail's pace.

Over time, my excitement about going to work gradually declined. Making a living selling jewelry is highly competitive, and all too often the frustration of not earning enough in commissions caused friction and bad feelings among the other salespeople. In addition, as is the case with practically all sales jobs, the markets are based on the whims of the fluctuating economy and whatever trends are fashionable at any given time. And then there was the constant need to update my list of clients. When my initial positive attitude I had during my long drive to and from work, as well as the uplifting atmosphere at my workplace, began to decline, I decided to again become my own boss.

A month after quitting my sales position at Littman Jewelers, I opened a consignment store in downtown Stroudsburg that included a small section for jewelry repair. I found a place in a nearby strip mall and made an eye-catching sign "Mr. G" for

Standing outside our consignment store.

Goworek because Mark Goworek is jewelry expert—the "G" was for his surname. Mark and I had a friend in New York who designed and made handcrafted jewelry. Because I needed a large stock on hand, I took on consignment $250,000 worth of this jeweler's rings, bracelets, and necklaces. Besides jewelry, my store offered antiques and paintings on glass, as well as my clothes that I was no longer wearing.

After I had operated the consignment store for two years, I traveled to Las Vegas to visit with Anna, who had earlier moved there from New York. While there, I spent a couple of days exploring the city and concluded that Las Vegas was a great place to sell and invest in real estate, as well as open a jewelry store. Sin City's fast pace and bright lights reminded me of Manhattan and surely was in stark contrast to traditional Stroudsburg, Pennsylvania.

When I was perusing the city, I walked into a jewelry store in downtown Las Vegas and asked the manager who was the best jeweler in area.

"Mordechai Yerushalmi," he said without hesitation. "He and his wife have been in the business for thirty-five years and have twenty-four stores throughout the United States."

"How can I meet him?"

"You could try calling him and making an appointment." He gave me Mordechai's phone number, and the following day I met with him at one of his ("The Jewelers") outlets that was located in the luxurious Mandalay Bay Hotel.

I was impressed from the second I walked into the store. A showcase of traditional and fine jewelry, gold, pearls and settings were beautifully arranged in gleaming showcases. Nearby were brilliant displays of Natalie K Elegant Collection, Scott Kay Vintage, Art carved Wedding Bands, and Tacori.

"You want to have the best jeweler working for you?" I asked the owner. "His name is Mark Goworek. He worked for the top jeweler in New York and we're moving to Las Vegas."

Mordechai was a meticulously dressed, handsome man with a warm smile.

"Okay," he said. "When you arrive and get settled, have Mr. Goworek contact me and I'll be happy to meet with him."

Upon my return to Stroudsburg, Mark and I sold the house, closed the consignment store, and sublet our lease. Two days later, we landed at McCarran International Airport in Las Vegas, moved into a nice home, and by the end of the week Mark had met with the owner of "The Jewelers" and was hired on the spot.

After completing a brush-up course in real estate, I passed the Nevada real estate test and was issued my real estate license in October of 2004. After working in real estate for a year and establishing a great rapport with growing list of return clients, I took a second job at McCarran International Airport as a hostess in its VIP lounge.

While I loved being with real estate clients, the majority of them were residents of Las Vegas, and I missed the diversity of people I regularly met when I worked as a manicurist in New York. Working at McCarran's VIP lounge allowed me to mingle with a wide variety of passengers on incoming and outgoing flights—including film and television celebrities, Las Vegas mainline entertainers, business executives and entrepreneurs, and politicians and dignitaries.

Another couple of years passed. Life was beautiful and business was booming. On all fronts I was on the top of my game.

Then one sunny afternoon, I was stopped at a busy Las Vegas intersection. When the light changed, the driver of the SUV in front of me proceeded into the intersection where a car suddenly pulled in front of him, cutting him off. The SUV driver slammed on his brakes and narrowly avoided an accident. As I stopped behind the SUV, I looked in my rearview mirror and saw a car coming at me full speed. Knowing I was going to be hit, I braced as the car slammed into the back of my new Volkswagen Jetta.

Moments after I realized I'd been in an accident, I stepped from my car and walked to the woman driver of the car behind me. I was furious. I tried to open the driver's door because I honestly wanted to beat her up for destroying my new car, but the

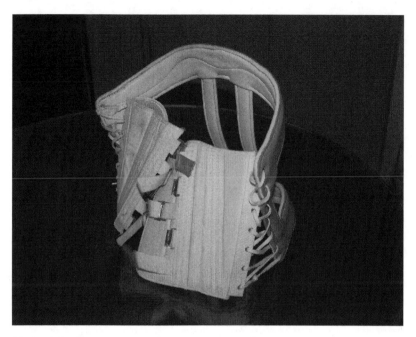

My back brace.

door was jammed and wouldn't open. At the time, I wasn't feeling any pain because of the adrenalin rush.

Five minutes later, the police and paramedics arrived and determined that I was the only one who was injured. I declined being taken to the hospital because I was worried that the police were going to tow my car, and I was embarrassed that, when my car was hit, I had wet my pants. Because the paramedics were concerned about my injuries, the police insisted that I go to the emergency room. After examining me at the hospital, the doctors found that I had injured my ribs and had bruises on my brain.

"I have a brain?" I said jokingly. Dating back to my childhood, I often joked when I was nervous. I soon learned that my condition was anything but a laughing matter.

Over the next two weeks, I underwent tests that revealed that my most serious problem was that the accident had injured my back. As a result, in order to stabilize my spine, it was necessary for me to wear a back brace that I disguised by wearing loose clothing.

LEFT: My father Bruno. BELOW: With my granddaughter Kinga and Dr. Ddad who saved my life when I had appendicitis.

This brace was tremendously helpful when it was on, but at night, after a month, I had more pain in my back when I took the brace off. Moreover, my stomach and lower back muscles had atrophied considerably because of my constantly wearing the brace.

When my pain became unbearable, the doctors prescribed the opiate Oxycotin that I took five times a day. Prior to my accident, I'd never taken drugs. Due to the regular dosage of Oxycotin, it was necessary for Anna to drive me to appointments because I was not permitted to drive.

On a fairly regular basis, my medication caused me to become so drowsy that I needed to lie down and sleep and, as a result, I lost my jobs at the airport and my real estate sales position. I'd become a vegetable that was little use to anyone, and there were times when I wanted to die.

After being under the care of a group of physicians for several months without improvement, the doctors advised me to undergo a series of operations. I was terrified because I'd heard numerous horror stories about botched back operations, but soon accepted the fact that I had no other options. Besides having incurred neurological problems and bruises on my brain and a back problem that required bone transplants, whenever I sneezed, I peed. When I was initially examined by a doctor, he told me that I needed a lawyer.

"Why?" I asked. I assumed that my insurance company, as well as the insurance company of the driver who had hit me, was paying my medical bills and to replace my car.

"Because the specialist I'm going to refer you to won't see anyone who isn't represented by an attorney."

"All I want is a good doctor," I kept saying, but my insistence fell on deaf ears.

The lawyer I was referred to looked like he worked for the Italian mafia. I stayed five minutes and left. Later that week, an attorney named Patrick Murphy, who was a friend, saw me limping into a supermarket and asked what had happened to me. When I told him about my car accident, he encouraged me to retain legal representation and convinced me to let him handle my case. The following week, I met with him at his office.

"Don't spend too much time on this," I said, "because I don't think we're going to get anything." I had nothing concrete to substantiate this. It was just a feeling.

"Do you understand what's ahead of you? You're going to have back surgery. After your surgery you're not going to be the same. You won't be able to ski or skate. You're going to be a cripple."

"Sounds like a great future."

We went back and forth about his representing me, and I finally agreed to allow him to pursue my case.

The day before I began a series operations, I drove to Valley Hospital because I wanted to see the outside of the hospital where I was going to die. I honestly believed that I wouldn't leave that hospital alive because I could no longer tolerate the intense pain I was living with, as well as the daily high dosage of drugs I was forced to take.

X-rays of my spine showing stabalizing pins.

Around Easter of 2009, I underwent the first stage of the operation that centered on repairing my damaged ribs and re-aligning my ribcage and spine. The following day, I underwent a second procedure during which the surgeons inserted stabilizing screws and wires into my ribs and spinal discs. Then the follow-ing "day three" of my multi-staged operation, the surgeons were scheduled to operate on my back, but my pain was unbearable and I told them to forget it. Anna stood firm at my bedside and insisted, "Momma, if you don't let the doctors do this operation, you're going to die."

"Fine," I said. "It's springtime. Flowers are cheap."

Anna went to my nurse and told her that I was being impossi-ble. Apparently, they all banded together and hit me with enough sedation to put down a charging bull elephant. The next thing I knew, I opened my eyes and looked up at Anna, who told me that the operation was over.

"I know," I said groggily, assuming she was referring to my second operation. When Anna finally managed to convey to me that I successfully underwent the third and final stage of my op-eration, I said, "Oh my god, thank you! I'm still alive!"

Late that night when I was alone in my hospital room, I was suddenly awakened by a strong sense of my mother's presence. I had felt no connection to her since her passing several years ear-lier. But now she was here. I didn't see her physical presence, but heard her voice—not in my room, but in the deepest part of my inner being. The sound of her voice was like none other, softly telling me, "Calm down. Relax. Take care of your health. I am here. Everything is going to be okay," just like she had told me so many times over the telephone.

During my recovery, besides Anna, my best friend Mark was a real trooper. He came to my hospital room every day before going to work and brought me my favorite fresh carrot juice and homemade chicken soup. After checking with the nursing staff to make sure I had everything I needed, he went off to work. Then immediately following work, he would return to my hospital room. On several difficult nights, he would spend the night sleeping in a chair beside my bed. I felt extremely blessed to have him in my life during this most difficult time. He has been my best friend for many years and is a shining example of a true helpmate.

With Mark Goworek.

After two weeks, the doctors released me from the hospital and sent me home. Although my ability to stand and walk had improved, I was still fighting with pain. Then one morning, a smart Jewish doctor that I began seeing told me to throw away all those medications the other physicians had prescribed, and he started giving me a small amount of morphine every two hours. It was a miracle. After five days, I felt as if I'd never had back surgery. A week later, I hiked up a hill. It took me two hours to get to the top of that hill, but I made it. Moments after I arrived at the top, my nephew Matthew, who was visiting from London, took a victory snapshot.

I was feeling better than I had in months when I arrived for my appointment with my attorney Patrick Murphy that had been scheduled weeks earlier. When I told the receptionist my name, she scanned her computer, then looked back at me. "When do you have an appointment?" she asked.

"This morning. Nine a.m. with Patrick Murphy."

The woman hesitated as she swallowed hard and then said, "Patrick is dead."

At first I thought I hadn't heard right. Or had I? "What are you talking about?" I said. "I have an appointment with him. He's not dead."

The woman could tell I was upset and asked me to sit down. I was to hear yet another one of life's rude twists and turns. Patrick Murphy was only 50 years of age when he traveled to his favorite haunt in Costa Rica for a vacation. Then one night, he went to bed and never woke up, having died in his sleep from a heart attack. The woman told me that Mr. Murphy's assistant secretary had left a message on my answering machine regarding Mr. Murphy's death, but apparently I hadn't received it.

Patrick Murphy's office referred me to another attorney who, after weeks of negotiations with the insurance company that represented the woman driver who had hit me, settled my claim. Unfortunately, although the woman's insurance paid all my medical bills, legal fees, and replaced my car, there wasn't enough left in the policy for my pain and suffering. And as is often the case in such legal matters, the woman who hit me had no personal assets to attach and was living from paycheck to paycheck. Looking on the bright side, the ordeal was finally over and I felt blessed and fortunate to be alive—and with the full belief that the best is yet to come.

CHAPTER THIRTEEN

DESIGN FOR LIVING

A wise man once said that the key to immortality is living a life worth remembering. I'd like to think that, thus far, I've lived such a life. I say "thus far" because I am confident that I still have a fair amount of quality living to do.

Another great man, Andy Rooney, once said that the best classroom in the world is at the feet of an elderly person. And yes, although I still feel young and am in excellent health, I'm aware of the reality of Father Time and the words of a dear golfing friend who now and then quips that "Say what you will, but you're still on the back nine." In any case, what follows are the lessons in life that I've learned and that I have enjoyed sharing with others, especially my children and grandchildren.

After living life for slightly more than seven decades, I have no doubt that, from the cradle to the grave, the most important aspect of life is family. One of dozens of wise old sayings that I love is "One chimpanzee is no chimpanzee," which means that we need other humans in order to feel and live our humanness. This starts with family, with our mother and father, siblings, grandparents, aunts and uncles, cousins, and on down the line of relatives. These are the people with whom we first learn about the most valuable assets in life—how to love and trust. Children who learn to love and trust their family then walk through life with the ability to love and trust others.

A highly brilliant and perceptive Beverly Hills psychiatrist once stated that a key question that he asks his patients early on in their therapy is "When you were young and growing up, who loved you?" To me, this is a profound question. I cannot fathom what life would be like for a child who felt unloved. Throughout my life I have felt incredibly fortunate that I was loved by so many of my key family members, especially my mother and my grandmother Emily, as well as my sisters. What a truly wonderful treasure their undying love has been.

My family has been my rock solid foundation because I have always known that my parents loved and valued me, and because of this they took good care of me and worried about me constantly. In return, I have from as early back as I can remember done my best to honor their great sacrifices by becoming the best person I could possibly be. When at times in my life I have reflected on what my parents went through escaping from the Nazi ghetto in Bialystok—and especially the dangerous risks that my mother took so that I would be born—I have been brought to tears. Because of the sacrifices that most parents make, I feel that children need to work their hardest to reach their highest goals in life in order to make their parents proud. I know that both of my daughters have done this for me, whether or not this was their intention, and I'd like to think that my parents were proud of me. As an important footnote, to give credit where credit is due, all of my successes in life are the result of the countless hours my parents spent preparing me for life.

When it comes to those we love, there is no sacrifice that is too big or too small. The first time I was faced with this challenge was when I learned of my first husband's heart condition and that he would need to have a life-saving surgery. Practically from the moment I learned of this, I made every effort to make this become a reality. Besides quitting college and devoting myself to working hard with no vacation in order to help pay for this procedure, I stopped at nothing to find the best heart surgeon in the world. I simply would not accept no for an answer and was willing to make any and all sacrifices to restore Andrew's health.

Years later, when I felt that the Soviet Union was going to invade Poland, I happily made whatever sacrifices were necessary to make preparations to bring my family to America. I had no

A fine grouping of with Anna, Jolanta, and my mother.

problem making these sacrifices because my parents had made similar sacrifices for me. For them, as was for me (and I know for my two daughters with their children) there is no sacrifice too big or too small. What an extraordinarily valuable gift this is to pass on to our children.

One key exception to this is one cannot make sacrifices for people they care about that they know will ultimately end in a negative outcome. I learned this important lesson in life from my marriage to Richard Cantarella. Although he initially was aware of my desire to become a successful businessperson, as I was in Poland, soon after we were married, he was determined that I take on the role of a stay-at-home housewife. In addition, he wanted me to continue living in Rahway, which was a place that I adamantly made clear would cause me considerable unhappiness. Although I initially agreed to make these sacrifices for Richard Cantarella, I knew in my heart that these sacrifices would not have a positive result. Following my basic instinct and not agreeing to his wishes when he first made them would have ultimately saved both of us a considerable amount of unhappiness. Throughout my life, I have refused to live under any form of oppression whether this oppression came from an entire country like the Soviet Union or an individual. The brilliant Dr. Wayne Dyer summed this up quite well when he said, "There is no such thing as a well-adjusted slave. You cannot get to a sense of purpose and live a life of harmony and balance while simultaneously allowing someone else to dictate your thoughts and actions."

As far back as I can remember, I have felt the need to march to the beat of my own drum. This isn't to say that I insist on being my own boss and that I don't accept guidance from others because I believe that I am often guided by an inner feeling that comes from deep inside. This process is best described by the old adage (author unknown) "That which you are seeking is causing you to seek." One of the best examples of this was when in 1987 I first traveled to the United States. While there were a half dozen places for me to emigrate to—Italy, Spain, England, and Australia, for example—I felt strongly drawn to America. It was almost like I was being pulled by a giant magnet. So it came as no surprise when I arrived in New York and found the city to be profoundly familiar, as if I'd been there before. It was as if the vibrations and essence of New York had been causing me to seek New York.

I think it's important to live one's life to the fullest. We are here for such a short time, and we owe it to ourselves to accomplish as much as we can and to enjoy all that life has to offer. As was written in the first pages of this book, there is a wonderful passage from *The Gitanjali* by Rabindranath Tagore that says, "The song you came to sing remains unsung to this day for you have spent all of my days stringing and unstringing your instrument." I never wanted to be someone who was constantly tuning up but never playing my song. Even as a young child, I loved walking through the park alone at night singing. I've always loved to sing and dance because they both touch a deep place in my heart. And so I think people have to pursue their dreams with all that they have. Even if these dreams don't come true, the journey itself is immensely rewarding.

Another important lesson that I've often shared either through words or by example is that throughout my life I've tried to not compare myself to others. The only person I compare myself to is me; to ask myself at the end of each day, "How am I doing today compared to yesterday or last week or even last year?"

When I was young and competing in sports, the other athletes who were entered in the race along with me weren't my true competition. Instead, what they served was they caused me to run the fastest race that I could run. When I crossed the finish line ahead of everyone else, my only question was had I broken my previous best time? After that, I wondered if I had broken someone else's best time and even set a new record. There's an old adage that says, "If you can't win the race, make the runner ahead of you break the record." And so those other athletes really weren't my competition. They were what spurred me on to be the best that I could be.

I have always been a firm believer in having a plan—or blue-print—for defining and achieving my goals. After my husband Andrew passed away, I could not have continued to operate our chicken farm without a detailed plan that I followed religiously every day. Besides sticking to this plan, at the end of each day I meticulously went over every aspect of the farm's operation and made changes to the plan where I felt changes were needed.

The same was true once I determined what I needed to achieve in New York, to establish roots so that I could bring my family to America. Having decided that becoming a cosmetologist and perfecting my English would lead to a successful career, I enrolled in classes that would make this dream come true. When I decided to form my *Design for Life* school, I enrolled in etiquette school and graduated from a class in interior decorating. When Leona Helmsley planted the seed about my getting into real estate, I took the necessary steps to become a licensed realtor. Goals are attained and dreams come true when one has a realistic plan and sticks to that plan with undying hope and determination. My mother's bravery and determination to become reunited with my father after they had both escaped the Nazi ghetto taught me these things at an early age.

I think that everyone needs to establish a set of simple basics that they will bring to all of life's endeavors. For me, these simple basics were: (1) I would be a hard worker, (2) that I would live by a standard of good morals and ethics in both my personal and business relationships, (3) that I would be well groomed, have nicely pressed clothes, and wear pleasant perfume, (4) that I would be on time and never keep anyone waiting, and (5) that no matter where I lived, even if in a tiny single room apartment, it would be located in a nicely kept, respectable neighborhood.

From the time I was a small child, my mother taught me never to lie and to be totally frank and honest with everyone I met. She'd say that if I lied, the next step would be that I would kill someone. I don't think she literally meant such a quantum leap. What she meant was that if I was willing to hedge on my moral-

My beautiful daughter Jolanta.

My lovely daughter Anna.

ity, then it would begin a process of eventual erosion of my sense of right and wrong that ultimately could end up with my committing even the most serious of immoral acts. My mother was a strong believer in truth and honesty. She would have completely agreed with the wise words of attorney Gerry Spence who once said, "We need to stay close to the truth, because when we don't, half-truths soon become whole lies."

Another important life principle that I was taught by my mother was that I should always do my best work and to not take on any project or set any goal unless I was willing to put forth my best effort. It was because of this principle that I was able to become successful at the highly detailed profession of a manicurist. Those who are employed in the best salons in Manhattan have to be meticulous about their work because they are grooming some of the most influential and wealthy people in the world—and these people expect perfection.

I've also learned that it's okay to take chances when you know you're in the right and on the right path. When I've found myself up against major challenges and seemingly against heavy odds, there seemed to be a nod of approval from the universe when I forged ahead with total and complete confidence. Heavy rains have reminded me of challenges in life. I never asked for a lighter rain. I just prayed for a better umbrella. Meeting life's challenges is really all about attitude.

I could have never come as far as I have had it not been for the care and protection of a group of role models and mentors. My mother was my stronger pillar who never once let me down. In my brightest and darkest hours she was always there with me. There was nothing she would not sacrifice if she felt it would help me. Collectively all of the lessons she taught me have provided me with the tools that have made all my dreams come true. For this I shall be eternally grateful. I owe her a debt that I can never repay.

Besides my mother, I have been blessed to have learned from business giants like Leona Helmsley, Victor Potamkin, Leon Hess, and Robert Tisch, to name but a few. In addition to being a mentor, Mr. Victor was my protector, as were several other individuals. And of course, I've been blessed to have my best friend and helpmate Mark Goworek in my life for more than two decades. When I went to bed at night, I often slept like a baby, knowing that there were people who truly cared about me and were there to protect me even when I slept—and most importantly knowing they would still be there when I awoke.

One of the hardest things I've had to learn is getting used to surprises. Life is full of them. If it wasn't, life would be monotonous and predictable. Surprises are also what make us feel the full force of our emotions, whether the sudden sheer joy from discovering that you've won the lottery or the utter despair upon learning that a loved one has died in a tragic car accident. Sudden deaths are the hardest for most people. I never anticipated the death of my first husband, or the sudden deaths of my infant son, my sister Halina, my mother, and even the sudden death of my attorney Patrick Murphy.

Of course the unexpected, serendipitous high points in life are welcomed with exuberance, and are sometimes looked upon as God-given blessings. The point is, these extreme shock moments in life are going to happen. There is just no way around this. And so one needs to accept that these resultant huge emotional swings are simply a necessary part of experiencing life.

How much easier life would be if we knew the exact hour that we—and our loved ones—were going to die. With the rare exceptions, however, of physician assisted suicide and capital punishment cases, knowing the hour of our death isn't part of the universal design. As such, it is vitally important to recognize that on any given day when we say goodbye to a friend or loved one—either by letter, telephone, or in person—that this could be the last communication we have with them. It takes only an extra moment to let them know how much we value them and how blessed we feel that they are an important and treasured part of our lives.

I am a strong believer in spiritual guides and guardian angels, and the notion that in times of life-altering distress I'm not alone has been comforting. When I traveled by ship to Sweden after my first husband Andrew passed away, he had told me earlier that if anything happened to him that he wanted me to remarry. So when I met the ship captain and discovered that his name was Andrew, I honestly believed that my deceased husband had a part in arranging this serendipitous meeting. Moreover, after my mother died and I was in the hospital recovering from surgery, I truly felt her presence one night and received her comforting assurance that everything was going to be fine. Although I didn't literally hear her voice, there was no question that she was present and that I clearly understood her message.

From an early age I learned from my mother that giving is far better than receiving. Although most of my childhood friends didn't agree with this, especially around Christmas time, for me this came naturally. I can still recall when I was a kid earning money by cleaning up the frontyards of neighbors so that I could buy my sisters pretty beads and dresses and show them off as we walked together down the main street in Bialystok. When my daughter Anna spent much of her free time working at the Harmonie Club, I was beaming with pride when she sent her entire earnings of $3,000 to her sister in Poland to help purchase a condominium.

On a much larger scale, Mr. Hess and Victor Potamkin were well known for their enormous generosity that they extended to friends and loved ones, charities, and even to total strangers. They are both shining examples of the peace of mind and sheer joy that comes from giving without expecting anything in return.

There is tremendous rise in self-esteem that comes to those who pay their own way in life, or at least try their best to pay their fair share. I learned this from my mother, who for most of her life worked from sunup to sundown. With the exception of the time I was recovering from my car accident, I don't recall a time in my adult years when I wasn't working.

Sometimes an individual can pay their own way by contributing their time volunteering. While they don't receive actual money for their work, they receive the joy of having contributed something of a positive nature to society. Sometimes the rewards that we receive are far more personal in nature. I would have worked for Victor Potamkin for free because of all his mentoring and caring that he added to my life, in addition to my feeling important because he felt that I was capable of handling so many important things in his life and that he trusted me implicitly.

Of all the negative emotions we're wired for, in my view the negative emotion of anger is by far the most self-destructive. While I recognize that there are times when anger in the form of venting has had a short-term positive effect on my well-being, I cannot remain angry at anyone, including God, for long. The only valuable purpose that anger serves is that it alerts us to whatever it is that's causing us emotional pain. Anger is like a car's warning light that alerts us that if the engine is fixed soon that a far more serious problem will result. Ironically, in the majority of times in my life when I have felt angry, when I finally thought it through, I realized that I had misread the real problem and discovered that what had initially bothered me really had nothing to do with me. And so oftentimes anger is simply a voice in our ear that tells us that we have to stop and think something through, analyze the problem, and then take action to repair the problem before it leads to a more serious situation.

Another great lesson that I've learned is that words spoken out of anger are often far more hurtful than an act of physical violence. When my father came into my bedroom and learned of my marriage to Andrew, he spent what seemed an eternity calling me an assortment of hurtful names. I can still recall thinking that I would have much preferred that he beat me with his belt. I felt the same way when Richard Cantarella called Polish people stupid and when that woman at the Yale Club whispered to her friend while indicating me, "Who's she?" as if I didn't belong there. In most instances, the hurt caused by derogatory remarks stays with a person far longer than a physical slap in the face.

One of my favorite quotes is by Mark Twain who said that "Forgiveness is the fragrance the violet sheds on the boot that has crushed it." To me, forgiveness is what takes all the power away from anger, and when we sincerely forgive someone for their wrongdoing—or ask them to forgive us for ours—the mere act is an instant remedy. I honestly believe that one of the first lessons one needs to teach a child is about forgiveness. Once they embrace this and practice it in their daily living, life becomes far easier and rewarding.

Of all the positive attributes that person can possess, if I had to choose one that would best contribute to a long and happy life, it would be gratitude. In one of actor William Holden's westerns, he is in a bathhouse with another cowboy played by Ryan O'Neal. The two are relaxing in their hot bath tubs, drinking whiskey, and smiling now and then as they draw on cigars. Ryan asks Holden, "I wonder what the poor people are doing right now?" After giving it thought, the smile fades from Holden's face and he replies thoughtfully and succinctly, "Without."

That one word says so much about the a large majority of people who live in the world today and are living without a roof over their heads, clean water, clothing, and adequate food and medical care. Children have is far worse than adults. Every day, 27,000 children worldwide die from "doing without." And so each and every day I thank God for all my blessings, especially for all the loved ones I have in my life, and most of all for another day. For those who think it's their alarm clock that woke them up that morning, they should try putting their clock beside a dead body, and they will realize that it's the Grace of God that woke them up.

Finally, I'd like to close with what I believe is the best medicine in the world, beside prayer, when it comes to curing every illness of the body and soul—and that is laughter. Having gone through many serious illnesses in my life, I know this to be true. To further illustrate, I'd like to share the story of Norman Cousins who served as an Adjunct Professor of Medical Humanities for the School of Medicine at the University of California at Los Angeles. It was at UCLA that he conducted research on the bio-chemistry of human emotions, which he believed were the key to patients' success in fighting illness.

Told that he had little chance of recovery, Cousins developed a recovery program incorporating mega doses of Vitamin C, along with a positive attitude, love, faith, hope, and laughter induced by the legendary comedy films of the Marx Brothers. "I made a joyous discovery," Cousins said after his complete recovery, "that ten minutes of genuine belly laughter had an anesthetic effect and would give me at least two hours of pain-free sleep. When the pain-killing effect of laughter wore off, we would switch on the motion picture projector again and it would lead to another pain-free interval."

Comedic icon Milton "Uncle Miltie" Berle once said "Laugh-ter is an instant vacation" and Charlie Chaplin said "A day with-out laughter is a day wasted." Because we are all here for such a short time, we need to laugh and have fun with life—if for no other reason than life is surely going to have fun with us. I wish all who read this book a wonderful journey in life. Most of all, I hope that each one of you will "sing the song you came to sing."

About the Authors

JOLANTA SOYSAL was born and raised in Poland. In 1987, after living under martial law for six years and at the age of 43, she traveled to the United States where she resided in New York. Over the next decade, she became a highly successful cosmetologist, businessperson, and personal assistant to one of America's biggest financial tycoons. Having become a United States citizen in 1993, today she resides in Las Vegas, Nevada and often travels to Poland.

TOM BLEECKER began his writing career in 1969 as a screenwriter for director Blake Edwards. After nearly two decades writing for screen and television, in 1987 Bleecker co-authored his first book with Linda Lee, *The Bruce Lee Story*, which served as the source material for MCA Universal's motion picture *Drgaon*. In 1996, Bleecker wrote a second book on Lee, a highly controversial bestseller entitled *Unsettled Matters*. After penning nearly 50 biographies, in 2012 Bleecker wrote his first novel *Tea Money* that was followed by *Big Band Star Maker* (the life story of Big Band leader Horace Heidt). His last book, *The Jet: The Benny Urquidez Story*, was published in 2014. Bleecker lives with his wife Lourdes in Southern California.

www.tombleecker.com

Proof

Made in the USA
Charleston, SC
09 September 2015